Information and Recommender Systems

Advances in Information Systems Set

coordinated by
Camille Rosenthal-Sabroux

Volume 4

Information and Recommender Systems

Elsa Negre

WILEY

First published 2015 in Great Britain and the United States by ISTE Ltd and John Wiley & Sons, Inc.

ISTE Ltd
27-37 St George's Road
London SW19 4EU
UK

www.iste.co.uk

John Wiley & Sons, Inc.
111 River Street
Hoboken, NJ 07030
USA

www.wiley.com

Library of Congress Control Number: 2015948079

British Library Cataloguing-in-Publication Data
A CIP record for this book is available from the British Library
ISBN 978-1-84821-754-6

Contents

Introduction

The development of Web and communications technologies since the early 1990s has facilitated the generation of initiatives aiming to create opportunities for communication and information sharing. Information and data are increasingly present in our daily lives. This constant flux is often the result of developments in Information and Communication Technologies (ICT)[1]. Moreover, the possibilities offered by ICT, which have increased almost exponentially, have given rise to a massive volume of data requiring processing [BAT 13]. The world is increasingly "digital" and individuals are increasingly affected by these changes. The digital infrastructure has resulted in the creation of an information environment that is "as imperceptible to us as water is to a fish" [MCL 11]. A type of parallel exists between humans and technology: on the one hand, individuals are making increasing use of technology and becoming "hyper-connected", on the other hand, digital systems are becoming increasingly user-centered [VII 14].

Systems therefore need to allow users to synthesize information and to explore data. Data exploration is a process focused on the search for relevant information within a set of data, intended to detect hidden correlations or new information. In the current context of "information overload", and with the increase in calculation and storage capacity, it is difficult to know exactly what information to look for and where to look for it. There is therefore a

---

1 The notions of Information and Communication Technologies (ICT) and New Information and Communication Technologies (NICT) include techniques associated with computing, audiovisual, multimedia, the Internet and telecommunications, allowing users to communicate, access information sources and store, process, produce and transmit information in a variety of forms: text, music, sound, image, video and interactive graphical interfaces [WIK 15a].

need for computing techniques that make this search, and the extraction of relevant information, easier. A technique that may be used is recommendation.

The key question concerns the way to guide users in their exploration of data in order to find relevant information.

The recommendation process aims to guide users in their exploration of the large quantities of data available by identifying relevant information. It constitutes a specific form of information filtering, intended to present information items (films, music, books, images, Websites, etc.) that are likely to be of interest to the user. In general, the recommendation process aims to predict the user's "opinion" of each item, based on certain reference characteristics, and to recommend those items with the best "opinion" rating.

This book is structured as follows:

Chapter 1 introduces the notions inherent in systems that handle data and information. It aims to clarify ambiguities associated with information systems, decision support systems and recommender systems, before establishing a clear distinction between recommendation and personalization.

Chapter 2 presents the most widespread approaches used in presenting recommendations to users: content-based approaches, collaborative approaches, knowledge-based approaches and hybrid approaches.

Chapter 3 describes the different techniques used in recommender systems (similarities between users or items, analysis of relationships between users or items, classification of users or items, etc.).

The concepts presented in Chapters 1, 2 and 3 are illustrated in Chapter 4, showing how recommendation approaches and the associated techniques are used and implemented in practice across a variety of domains.

Chapter 5 presents different ways in which the quality of recommender systems can be evaluated.

Finally, the conclusion provides a summary of the book, with a presentation of the current challenges that need to be tackled.

Note that this book does not claim to provide an exhaustive and detailed list of all possible approaches and techniques, but it constitutes an introduction and overview of recommender systems and the way in which they operate.

A Few Important Details Before We Begin

Savoir pour prévoir, afin de pouvoir (Know in order to predict, and thus to act)
Auguste Comte, *Course of Positive Philosophy, 1830*

In computer science, the concept of information can have multiple meanings. However, most people agree that information is an item of knowledge that may be conserved, processed or communicated, and is thus linked to notions of communication, data, knowledge, meaning, representation, etc.

In this chapter, we aim to remove the ambiguities surrounding the terms "information system", "decision support system" and "recommender system", clearly establishing the relative positions of these different systems.

1.1. Information systems

For sustainable development, organizations need to respond to two key challenges: (i) management of an increasingly large quantity of data (both internal and external), enabling increasingly easy access, and (ii) transformation of this quantity of data into information that is useful for efficient accomplishment of their actions, while adapting to a continuously evolving environment.

An information system is an organized set of hardware, software, human resources, data, procedures, etc., which are used to collect, regroup, categorize, process and disseminate information in a given environment [DEC 92]. The general aim of an information system is thus to support an organization in achieving its objectives (essentially of a strategic nature).

Information systems are traditionally grouped into three types: design systems (Computer-Aided Design (CAD), etc.), industrial systems (management of machines, industrial process control, etc.) and management systems (marketing, human resources, etc.). We focus on the third type of system, which can also be split into two subcategories: operational information systems (used to carry out operations) and decision support systems.

Information therefore needs to be robust and durable, as it has an influence on company strategy, but also be able to evolve and adapt for different collaborators, processes, etc. This requirement often leads to the automation of decisions, in operational terms, and predictive analysis of evolutions, for strategic purposes. Real-time knowledge of both past and present situations is a key factor in ensuring the strategic success of companies.

Further details on information systems may be found in [ROS 09] (in French) and [STA 92] (in English).

1.2. Decision support systems

Unlike operational (or transactional) systems, which are specific to a company's activities and are intended to assist with everyday management tasks, decision support systems are used to facilitate the definition and implementation of strategies. However, the goal is not to define a strategy once and for all, but to be able to adapt to an environment in a continuous manner and in a better way than the competition. Traditional decision support systems are used to analyze activities that have already been performed in order to obtain information relevant to future activities; to do this, they use more or less recent information (in the best cases, this is updated daily). More advanced decision support systems manage more recent information (some are updated in quasi-real time), automate the decision process and provide real-time operational support (Internet call centers, for example) [BRU 11].

One of the best-known concepts encountered in decision support systems is the data warehouse. Often considered to be the core of any decision support system, a data warehouse integrates and stores significant volumes of data from a wide variety of sources:

– internal sources: software packages (Enterprise Resource Planning (ERP), Customer Relationship Management (CRM), etc.), databases, files, Web services, etc.;

– external sources (clients, suppliers, etc.);

– non-computerized sources (letters, memoranda, minutes of meetings, etc.);

in order to make these data easily accessible for querying and for the purposes of decision analysis. The data warehouse is defined as "a subject-oriented, integrated, time-variant, nonvolatile collection of data in support of managements decision-making process" [INM 94].

Further details on decision support systems and data warehouses may be found in [FER 13] (in French) and [KIM 02] (in English).

1.3. Recommender systems

Data exploration is a process that involves searching for relevant information, within a set of data, with the intention of detecting hidden correlations or new information. Users face ever-increasing quantities of information, due to increased calculation and storage capacity [LYM 03][1], which makes it increasingly difficult to know exactly what information to look for and where to look for it.

There is therefore a need for IT (Information Technology) techniques to facilitate this search process, along with the extraction of relevant information. One of these techniques is information recommendation. The main aim of this technique is to guide users in their exploration of data in order to obtain relevant information. This is done through the use of recommendation tools, with the intention of providing users with relevant information as quickly as possible. The recommendation process guides

---

1 The School of Information Management and Systems at the University of Berkeley, California, has been carrying out a study of the quantity of new information created each year since the year 2000. This study considers all newly created information, stored in a variety of formats (printed matter, magnetic and optical film), and seen or heard via four information source fluxes using electronic pathways (telephone, radio, television and the Internet). The study estimates the quantity of information newly created each year at approximately 2 exabytes per year (1 exabyte = 10^{18} bytes).

users in their exploration of quantities of available information by identifying items that appear to be relevant. This technique represents a specific form of information filtering, aiming to present items (movies, music, books, news, images, Websites, etc.) that are likely to be of interest to the user. Generally, based on certain reference characteristics[2], the recommendation process aims to predict the "opinion" a user will have of each item and to recommend items with the best predicted "opinion".

Note that in this context, a user may be an organization or a company. In these cases, a recommender system can assist organizations or companies in making strategic choices, by highlighting the most relevant information.

1.4. Comparisons

In this section, we have provided Table 1.1 for use in comparing three of the systems introduced earlier: operational information systems, decision support systems and recommender systems. This comparison is based on six criteria: the number of users, the data handled, the time period covered by the system, system objectives, the type of access to data and update frequency.

Operational information systems or recommender systems allow multiple users (employees and/or decision-makers) to handle dynamic data whereas decision support systems allow a limited number of selected users (i.e. decision-makers) to access mostly static data. Moreover, although operational systems make use of only small volumes of "current" data, decision support systems and recommender systems make use of both historical and current data (in large quantities) to forecast the future.

These three types of system, based on the same principle of transforming data into information, differ in a number of ways. This is essentially due to their differing aims: operational information systems allow the visualization of current data, and thus present information, whereas decision support systems are used for prediction purposes, thus assisting in the decision-making process. Recommender systems are used to guide users in accomplishing a task (note that user tasks may also include decision-making).

---

2 These characteristics may, for example, come from the information items themselves (a content-based approach) or from the social environment (collaborative filtering).

	Operational information system	Decision support system	Recommender system
Users	Many (employees)	Few (decision-makers)	Many (employees and decision-makers)
Data	Detailed Large volumes Internal (application-oriented) Dynamic	Aggregated Large volumes Internal and external (subject-oriented) Static	Detailed Internal and external Dynamic
Time	Present	Past/present to future	Past/present to future
Access	Small amounts of data (up-to-date)	Large amounts of data (historical)	Large amounts of data (or very small amounts of data)
Updated	Very regularly	Periodically	Very regularly
Objective	Visualization of state	Forecasting, projection and decision	Support users in carrying out tasks

Table 1.1. *Comparison table: operational information systems, decision support systems and recommender systems*

1.5. Recommendation versus personalization

It is important to differentiate between recommendation and personalization, which are often confused in a variety of domains.

1.5.1. *Recommendation*

From our perspective, a recommended item (movie, book, etc.) is a pre-existing item, for example taken from a set of previously viewed items in a database or a catalog. The recommended items may therefore be completely different from the initial items, as they are not necessarily taken from the same catalog, or intended for the same user; they may even present very different characteristics. In general terms, the recommendation approach, based on an initial set of items Q, returns a set of items Q' such that $Q' \subsetneq Q$ (in the sense of set theory).

EXAMPLE 1.1.– Suppose that a user, interested in the term APPLE, wishes to enlarge his or her library, essentially made up of cookery books. This set of books, which the user already possesses, constitutes our set Q. Possible recommendations might include cookery books (including apple-based recipes), but also books on gardening (describing, for example, the way to plant and care for apple trees) and on traveling (for example concerning the "Big Apple", New York City). This list forms our set of recommended books Q'. Note that the set of initial items (books in the library, mostly cookery books, Q) and the set of recommendations (containing cookery books, but also gardening and travel books, Q') have few shared characteristics.

1.5.2. *Personalization*

From our perspective, personalization corresponds more closely to inclusion. In the field of databases, for example, query personalization is considered as an addition of constraints, generated by the user's profile, for a given query; this results in the addition of selection conditions [KOU 04, BEL 05]. In more general terms, using a set of items Q, a personalized approach will return a set of items Q' such that the characteristics of Q' are included in that of Q, $Q' \subsetneq Q$ (in the sense of set theory).

EXAMPLE 1.2.– Suppose that the set of items Q to personalize consists of cookery books concerning recipes using apples and that the user's preferences apply only to desserts. The book most suited to the user's preferences (i.e. a personalized choice Q') would be, for example, a book of apple-based dessert recipes.

To conclude, in this chapter we have clearly shown the difference between an operational information system, a decision support system and a recommender system; we have also distinguished between the notions of recommendation and personalization. In the rest of this book, we shall consider one specific type of information system: recommender systems, which provide recommendations to assist users in the fulfillment of given tasks.

2

Recommender Systems

Nous avons une superbe aiguillette de boeuf mode en gelée. Je me permettrai de vous la recommander. Cest très bien. A moins que vous nayez envie du poulet à l'estragon, qui est très bien aussi (We have a superb aiguillette of jellied beef, which I would recommend. It's very good. Unless you would prefer our chicken with tarragon, which is also very good)

Jean Dutourd, *The Horrors of Love, 1963*

A recommender system is an information-filtering technique used to present the items of information (video, music, books, images, Websites, etc.) that may be of interest to the user (Figure 2.1).

Recommender systems reduce information overload
by estimating relevance

item	score
i1	0.9
i2	1
i3	0.3
...	...

Recommendation
component

Recommendation
list

Figure 2.1. *The recommender system seen as a black box [JAN 10]*

2.1. Introduction

Recommender systems have been studied in the context of a range of domains, including information retrieval [KEN 71, SAL 83, BAE 99], the Internet [BAE 04, WHI 07], e-commerce [SCH 01], Web usage mining [SRI 00, FU 02, PIE 03, BAE 05] and many others. The key problem addressed by recommendation may be summarized as an estimation of scores for items that have not yet been seen by a user. The number of items and the number of system users may be very high, making it difficult for every user to view every item or for each item to be evaluated by all users. A method is, therefore, required to estimate the scores for non-viewed items.

Intuitively, this evaluation is generally based on the scores given by a user to other items, and on other information, which is formally described later in the chapter. When it is possible to estimate the scores for non-evaluated items, the items with the highest scores may be recommended to the user. In more formal terms, [ADO 05] formulated the recommendation problem in the context of e-commerce as given in definition 2.1.

DEFINITION 2.1.– *Recommendation in e-commerce.*

Let C be the set of all users, I the set of all possible items that may be recommended (books, videos, restaurants, etc.) and u a function that measures the utility of an item i to the user c, that is u: $C \times I \rightarrow \mathbb{R}$.

Thus, for each user $c \in C$, we wish to select the item $i' \in I$ that has the maximum utility for the user: $\forall c \in C, i'_c = argmax_{i \in I} u(c, i)$.

In recommender systems, the utility of an item is generally represented by a score, which indicates a specific user's appreciation of a specific item.

EXAMPLE 2.1.– *In this example, the items are movies that four users, Arnaud, Patrick, Marie and Elsa, may have scored. For example user Arnaud gave the movie "Harry Potter" a score of 3 (of 10). This gives us the matrix $C \times I$:*

u(c,i)	Harry Potter	Ice Age	Ice Age 2	The Expendables	Welcome to the Sticks
Elsa		8		2	7
Marie	9	8		3	6
Arnaud	3	5		5	
Patrick	5	3		3	3

Note that each cell (c, i) in the matrix corresponds to the utility score assigned to the movie i by the user c.

The central problem for recommender systems lies in the fact that this utility value u is not usually defined across the whole space $C \times I$ but simply for a certain subset. This means that u must be extrapolated to the whole space $C \times I$. In recommender systems, utility is typically represented by scores and is defined, first, using items that have previously been evaluated by users. The recommender engine should, therefore, be able to predict the scores of the non-evaluated item × user combinations and to publish appropriate recommendations based on these predictions.

Once unknown scores have been estimated, actual recommendations of items for a user are produced, choosing the highest score from the predicted scores for the specific user, following the formula given in definition 2.1.

The best items may be recommended to a user, that is the most relevant items for that specific user will be given; alternatively, a set of users may be recommended for an item, that is those most interested in the item will be named.

2.2. Classification of recommender systems

Recommender systems may be classified according to three approaches: score estimation method, the data used to estimate scores or the main objective of the system.

2.2.1. *Classification by score estimation method*

Unknown scores may be extrapolated from known scores via a heuristic or a model:

– heuristic[1]: a heuristic is specified to define the utility function and its execution is validated empirically. A utility function is then calculated to optimize certain execution criteria;

EXAMPLE 2.2.– *Consider the Users × Movies matrix from Example 2.1. One possible heuristic would be: value("Ice Age 2") = value("Ice Age") + 1. On the basis of this heuristic, the system gives the movie "Ice Age 2" values of 9 for Elsa and Marie, 6 for Arnaud and 4 for Patrick.*

– model: the collection of scores is used to "learn[2]" a model, which is then used to predict scores, whether via a probabilistic approach [BRE 98], automatic learning techniques [BIL 98] or statistical models [UNG 98].

EXAMPLE 2.3.– *Consider the Users × Movies matrix shown in Example 2.1. One example of a model consists of considering that all users providing evaluations for the movie "Welcome to the Sticks" gave a similar score to the movie "Ice Age 2". On the basis of this model, the system gives the movie "Ice Age 2" a score of 7 for Elsa, 6 for Marie and 3 for Patrick.*

2.2.2. *Classification by data exploitation*

Recommender systems may be classified according to the scores, which have already been evaluated, used to estimate the missing scores [HIL 95, BAL 97, KAZ 06]:

– content-based method: the user receives recommendations for items that are similar (in terms of a measure of similarity between the two items) to those which he or she has given high scores previously;

EXAMPLE 2.4.– *Consider the Users × Movies matrix shown in Example 2.1. The system attributes utility values to movies that Elsa has not yet evaluated. This utility value is calculated on the basis of scores given to the movies Elsa has already evaluated. The movies "Ice Age" and "Welcome to the Sticks" were scored in almost exactly the same way. On the basis of this observation and on the fact that the movies "Ice Age" and "Ice Age 2" are very "similar", for Elsa, the system gives the movie "Ice Age 2" the highest*

---

1 A heuristic is a problem-solving method that is not based on a formal model and will not necessarily produce an optimal solution.
2 A model may be learned via a learning sample. More precisely, models are constructed through the use of a learning sample and validated using a test sample.

score, which she gave to the movies "Ice Age" and "Welcome to the Sticks", that is 8.

– collaborative filtering method: the user receives recommendations for items that have received high ratings from other users with similar tastes and preferences (in terms of a measure of similarity between users and items);

EXAMPLE 2.5.– *Again, let us consider the Users × Movies matrix from Example 2.1. The system looks for users who are similar to Elsa: Marie is selected, as the two users gave very similar scores to the same movies. On the basis of Marie's scores, the system gives the movie "Harry Potter" a rating of 9 for Elsa, that is the score that Marie gave for the same movie.*

– hybrid method: a combination of the earlier-described two methods.

2.2.3. Classification by objective

Another method for classifying recommender systems was recently put forward by [HER 08], based on the objective of the recommender system rather than on the data or estimation methods used.

The author introduced two notions, *filter* and *guide*. The *filter* is responsible for selecting interesting or useful items from a large quantity of possible items, that is must identify candidates (useful/relevant items) and recommendable items. The *guide* is responsible for ordering recommended items, that is determining when and how each recommendation is to be presented to the user.

The *filter*, therefore, corresponds to the selection of candidates for recommendation from a large set of items, and the *guide* orders candidate recommendations.

In summary, the recommender systems assist users with information retrieval. Whatever is the system used, it may be classified on the basis of objective, the data used to estimate scores or the score estimation method.

2.3. User profiles

Whatever recommendation technique is used, certain information needs to be considered in relation to users; this information is stored in, what we call, user profiles. These profiles are constructed with or without input from the users themselves: a distinction is made between explicit and implicit data collection in the context of profile construction.

Data collection is explicit in cases in which the users explicitly express an opinion, for example by ordering a collection of items by preferences, choosing the most relevant item or creating a list of items that are interesting to them. Implicit data collection occurs when user preferences or opinions are induced by "analyzing" their actions, for example by considering which items the user has already seen, keeping track of browsing history (purchases, items considered for a certain period, etc.) and analyzing the user's social network to discover their likes and dislikes.

Further details on user profiles may be found in [BOH 07], [DAO 08] and [TCH 12] (in French), and [LAH 03] and [BHA 91] (in English).

Note that user profile data may be represented in different ways according to requirements but are generally stored as attribute–value pairs, in which each pair constitutes a property of the profile. Properties may also be grouped into categories.

EXAMPLE 2.6.– *Table 2.1 shows an extract from the profile of user Marie based on the information and preferences provided by the user.*

Identifier		1
Personal information	User	Marie
	Sex	Female
Book	Genre	Thriller/Crime
	Author	S. King, M. Connelly
Movie	Genre	Children's, Animated, Comedy
	Director	G. Lucas

Table 2.1. *Extract from the user profile for Marie*

2.4. Data mining

Recommender systems traditionally make use of techniques taken from research areas such as Human–Computer Interfaces (HCI) or Information Retrieval. However, many of these approaches are based on data mining techniques. This process involves three stages, according to [RIC 11]: preprocessing [PYL 99], analysis and interpretation of results (see Figure 2.2).

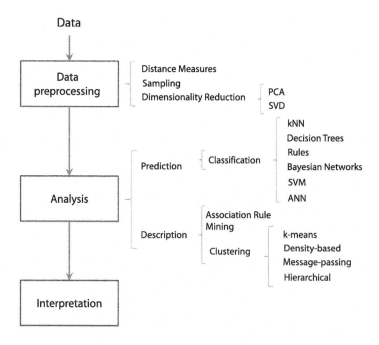

Figure 2.2. *Stages and methods used in approaches based on data mining [RIC 11]*

Data preprocessing (e.g. cleaning, filtering and transformation) is often necessary to obtain "clean" data, suitable for the analytical techniques used later. The most widespread preprocessing techniques are as follows:

– similarity measures or mathematical distance (which is presented in Chapter 3; examples include Euclidean distance, Cosine similarity and the Pearson correlation coefficient) to compare items;

– sampling, intended to provide a representative subset of a more voluminous initial set, for example cross-validation [ISA 08];

– dimension reduction (e.g. Principal Component Analysis (PCA) [HUA 04] or Singular Value Decomposition (SVD) [GOL 70]) to eliminate irrelevant and redundant information, reduce the dimensions of the Users × Items matrix and make the data set more representative of the problem.

Data analysis involves two distinct objectives: either predictive or descriptive. In the first case, classification techniques are used (k-Nearest

Neighbors (kNN) [COV 06], decision trees [QUI 86, ROK 08], rules [GUT 00], Bayesian networks [FRI 97], Support Vector Machines (SVM) [CRI 00] or artificial Neural Networks (aNN) [ZUR 92]). In the second case, the techniques used are based on association rules [MAN 94], clustering[3] (k-means [HAR 79], density-based [EST 96], message-passing-based [FRE 07] or using hierarchical approaches [OLS 95]).

2.5. Content-based approaches

For content-based approaches (see [PAZ 07] for further details), the system attempts to recommend items that correspond to the user's profile. The profile is generally based on items that the user has liked in the past or on interests explicitly defined by the user. A content-based recommender system matches the characteristics of an item to a user's profile to determine the relevance of the item for that particular user. The recommendation process thus consists of determining which items most closely match the user's preferences. This type of approach does not require a large community of users, or a long history of system use. This process is shown in Figure 2.3.

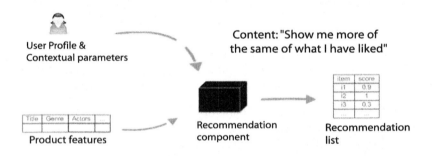

Figure 2.3. *Content-based recommender system seen as a black box [JAN 10]*

The simplest means of describing a catalog of items is to use an explicit list of the characteristics of each item (also known as attributes, item profiles, etc.). For a book, for example this might include the genre, author

---

3 Clustering consists of seeking a means of partitioning or grouping items into clusters or categories. This is done by optimizing a criterion that aims to group items into clusters, each of which should be as homogeneous as possible, and as distinct as possible from the other clusters.

name(s), publisher or any other information relating to the book. These characteristics are then stored, for example in a database. When a user profile is expressed in the form of a list of interests based on the same characteristics, the recommender system must simply match up the item characteristics with the user profile.

The degree of matching between the item characteristics and the user profile may be measured in a number of different ways, including the Dice index [DIC 45] or other similarity measures [BAE 99], the term frequency–inverse document frequency (TF-IDF) [SAL 75], techniques based on the similarity of vectorial spaces (kNN) [BIL 00], the Rocchio method [ROC 71], Bayesian approaches [PAZ 07], decision trees [QUI 93], etc. These methods are then combined with statistical techniques, such as χ^2 [CHU 93], in cases in which there are too many keywords. Note that some of these approaches are discussed in detail in Chapter 3.

Content-based recommender systems have a certain number of advantages:

– they recommend items similar to those that users have liked in the past;

– they take account of user profiles, something that is essential in order to obtain the most relevant recommendations for a specific user;

– the process of matching the user preferences with the item characteristics works for a large number of data types (text, digital, etc.) because of the use of keyword lists;

– data relating to other users are not required;

– there are no problems associated with "cold start[4]" as the method is based on matching the user preferences with the item characteristics;

– suitable recommendations can be made for users with "unique" tastes;

– new items or even unpopular items may still be recommended.

However, these systems also have their disadvantages:

– not all content may be represented using keywords (e.g. images);

---

4 Although recommender systems allow us to recommend relevant items to a user, problems arise when new items are added to the catalog, or in the case of new or different users. The cold start problem occurs when recommendations are needed for items and/or users where no implicit or explicit information is available. There are therefore two types of problem associated with cold start: new users and new products.

– it is not possible to distinguish between the items using the same sets of keywords;

– users who have already seen a large number of items are difficult to deal with (too much profile information to match with the item characteristics);

– no history is available when new users begin using the system;

– there is a risk of over-specialization, that is limiting recommendations to similar items (excessively homogeneous responses);

– user profiles remain difficult to create, and it is important to take account of changing or evolving tastes;

– the users need to provide feedback on suggestions in order to improve recommendation quality, something that is not generally appreciated;

– these systems are entirely based on item scores and interest scores: the fewer the available scores, the more the set of possible recommendations will be limited.

Note that not making use of other users' opinions represents both an advantage (little information is required) and a disadvantage (because of the lack of variety).

EXAMPLE 2.7.– *Let us consider a catalog of books, such as the extract presented in Table 2.2, and an extract from the profile of a specific user, Marie, based on previous book purchases and information provided concerning preferences, as shown in Table 2.3. We wish to recommend books that Marie might enjoy. To do this, we need to match up Table 2.2 with Table 2.3 and to identify those books that correspond most closely to Marie's preferences. Table 2.4 shows a summary of the matching process between the two tables (yes: details match; no: details do not match). Thus, from Table 2.4, we see that the books "The Shining" and "Millennium" could be recommended to Marie (as the characteristics of these books correspond most closely to Marie's preferences).*

Title	Genre	Author	Price	Keywords
Shining, The	Thriller	S. King	19.50	Alcoholism, Colorado, Mediums, Supernatural, Hotel, etc.
Millennium	Crime	S. Larsson	23.20	Journalism, Investigation, Murder, Sweden, Politics, etc.
Bridget Jones's Diary	Romance	H. Fielding	8.50	Single, Humor, Love, Thirty-something, Diary, etc.

Table 2.2. *Extract from a book catalog*

Titles	Genres	Authors	Price	Keywords
Doctor Sleep, Joyland, Suicide Intervention, Darling Lilly, etc.	Crime, Thriller	S. King, M. Connelly, etc.	15	Detectives, Murder, Supernatural, etc.

Table 2.3. *Extract from user profile: Marie*

User preferences	*The Shining*	*Millennium*	*Bridget Jones's Diary*
Genre	Yes	Yes	No
Price	Yes	Yes	Yes
Keywords	Yes	Yes	No

Table 2.4. *Matches between book characteristics and Marie's preferences (profile)*

2.6. Collaborative filtering approaches

The systems based on collaborative filtering (see [SCH 07] for more details) produce recommendations by calculating the similarity between the preferences of different users. These systems do not attempt to analyze or understand the content of recommended items but suggest new items to the users based on the opinions of the users with similar preferences. The method consists of making automatic predictions (filtering) regarding the interests of a given user by collecting the opinions of a large number of users. The hypothesis that underpins this type of approach is that those who liked a particular item in the past tend to continue to like this specific item (or very similar items). This process is shown in Figure 2.4.

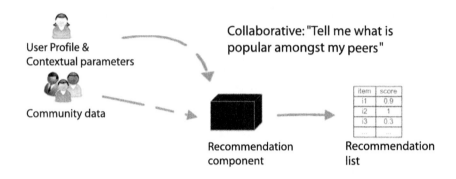

Figure 2.4. *Collaborative filtering recommender system seen as a black box [JAN 10]*

Collaborative approaches attempt to predict the opinion a user will have of different items and to recommend the "best" item to each user in relation to their previous tastes/opinions and the opinions of other similar users. This is generally done using the following mechanism:

1) Large numbers of user preferences are recorded.

2) A subset of users with similar preferences to the user seeking a recommendation is identified.

3) An *average* preference for this group is calculated.

4) The resulting preference function is used to recommend options/items to the user seeking a recommendation.

Note that the notion of similarity must be clearly defined.

Three approaches exist: item-to-item approaches, based on similarities between items; user-to-user approaches, based on similarities between users and other approaches. The difference between the first two approaches is shown in Example 2.8.

EXAMPLE 2.8.– *In this example, consider the Users × Movies matrix of Example 2.1, showing the scores given to movies by four users, Arnaud, Patrick, Marie and Elsa. For the purposes of this example, we shall simplify the matrix by replacing scores greater than or equal to 5 by a score of 1 and scores less than 5 by a score of 0. This gives us the following matrix:*

$u(c, i)$	Harry Potter	Ice Age	Ice Age 2	The Expendables	Welcome to the Sticks
Elsa		1		0	1
Marie	1	1		0	1
Arnaud	0	1		1	
Patrick	1	0		0	0

Using an item-to-item approach, recommendations are made by identifying items with the same level of interest for multiple users. Both Elsa and Marie like the movies "Ice Age" and "Welcome to the Sticks". This suggests that, as a general rule, users who like the movie "Ice Age" will also like "Welcome to the Sticks". The movie "Welcome to the Sticks" could, therefore, be recommended to Arnaud (who liked the movie "Ice Age"). Note that this approach is suitable for use with large numbers of users and items (into the millions).

In the case of a user-to-user approach, recommendations are produced by finding users with similar opinions. Both Elsa and Marie liked the movies "Ice Age" and "Welcome to the Sticks" but did not like "The Expendables". As Marie and Elsa share these opinions, it would appear that they generally have the same tastes. The movie "Harry Potter" would, therefore, be a good recommendation for Elsa, as Marie enjoyed it. Note that this approach would not be suitable for systems with millions of users.

Collaborative filtering recommender systems are extremely varied and may be based on a number of techniques, including:

– similarity between users (the Pearson correlation coefficient [ROD 88], etc.) or neighborhood selection (algorithms based on neighborhood searches (kNN [ADE 14], etc.)) for user-to-user approaches;

– similarity between items (Cosine similarity [QAM 10], etc.) for item-to-item approaches;

– score prediction techniques (PCA [PEA 01], matrix factorization (SVD [GOL 65]), Latent Semantic Analysis (LSA) [DEE 90], association rules, Bayesian approaches [FRI 97], etc.) for other approaches.

Note that some of these approaches are discussed in detail in Chapter 3.

Collaborative filtering recommender systems have a number of advantages:

– the use of other users' scores in evaluating the utility of items;

– identification of users or groups of users whose interests correspond to the current user;

– the more users the system has, the more scores will be available, thus improving result quality.

However, systems of this type also have their disadvantages:

– difficulty in identifying similar users or groups of users;

– the recommender system must deal with a low-density Users × Items matrix;

– the cold start problem is present for new users, as their preferences are unknown, and for new items added to the catalog, for which no scores will be available.

Note that in systems with large numbers of items and users, the calculation effort required increases in a linear manner; suitable algorithms are therefore required. Similarly, it is important to be aware of the problems associated with a lack of diversity: it is not particularly useful to recommend all movies starring the actor *Antonio Banderas* to a user who enjoyed one of his movies in the past. Finally, depending on the context in which the recommender system is used, that is according to the type of items, significant issues need to be managed, notably those relating to security and privacy.

2.7. Knowledge-based approaches

Knowledge-based recommender systems (see [BUR 00] for more details) are a specific type of recommender system based on explicit knowledge obtained by combining items, user preferences and recommendation criteria (concerning which items should be recommended in which context). These systems are applied in cases where alternative approaches, such as collaborative filtering or content-based approaches, cannot be applied. A major advantage of these systems is that the cold start problem does not exist in these cases. However, drawbacks exist concerning the acquisition of knowledge, which needs to be defined explicitly. Recommender systems of this type make use of information concerning users, items and the context. This process is shown in Figure 2.5.

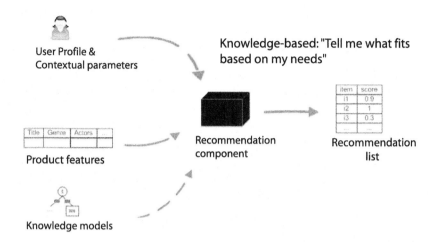

User Profile &
Contextual parameters

Knowledge-based: "Tell me what fits
based on my needs"

item	score
i1	0.9
i2	1
i3	0.3

Title	Genre	Actors	...

Product features

Recommendation
component

Recommendation
list

Knowledge models

Figure 2.5. *Knowledge-based recommender system seen as a black box [JAN 10]*

Two approaches are used in knowledge-based recommendation: case-based recommendation [BUR 00, SMY 04, MIR 05, RIC 07] and constraint-based recommendation [THO 04, FEL 07, FEL 08]. Systems of this type use a wide range of knowledge sources and operate in a very similar manner: for example they collect requirements from current users to propose new solutions or alternatives in cases where no solution can be identified and must be able to explain item recommendations.

Case-based recommenders consider recommendation as a similarity evaluation problem, aiming to find items that are most similar to the user's ideas, considering that similarity characteristics are often associated with domain-specific knowledge and considerations.

Constraint-based recommendations take account of explicitly defined constraints (for example filtering or incompatibility constraints).

If no items are found to correspond to the user's wishes (either the calculated similarity value is more than a certain threshold for all relevant items or the set of constraints and the user's wishes are contradictory), both the approaches use mechanisms to identify a minimum set of modifications to the user's wishes in order to obtain a solution [MCS 04, FEL 07]. Interactions with a knowledge-based recommender system are generally modeled in the form of a dialog box (conversational recommendation), in which users can specify their wishes in the form of responses to questions

[BUR 00, THO 04, MIR 05, FEL 07, RIC 07]. Interactions between the user and the application may also be enriched by the use of natural language [THO 04], which helps in more flexible interactions.

Many case-based recommendation applications use the concept of criticism [BUR 00, SMY 04, CHE 06], in which a given user answers to a recommended item by identifying the ways in which it differs from his/her ideal. For example, a user receiving a recommendation for a traditional-style restaurant may request a "more creative" option and will thus obtain a recommendation for an establishment offering a more contemporary take on the same style of cuisine [BUR 97]. This type of interface is helpful as it allows users to formulate requirements on the fly, in response to suggestions from the system.

However, certain types of items, such as apartments and cars, are not bought on a very regular basis; score-based systems, therefore, do not produce very good results because of the lack of available scores. In certain complex domains, clients wish to specify their preferences explicitly (e.g. the maximum price of a car). In this context, the recommender system needs to consider these constraints. For example, in the context of financial services, all suggestions should correspond to the investment period specified by the client. Aspects of this type are not considered by collaborative filtering or content-based approaches. In areas such as financial services, photography and tourism, only knowledge-based recommender systems are able to provide relevant recommendations.

Finally, knowledge-based recommender systems are often "conversational", that is user requirements and preferences are obtained through feedback. One major reason for the conversational nature of this type of recommender system is the complexity involved in accounting for all of a user's preferences at once. Furthermore, the user preferences are generally not precisely known at the outset but are constructed on the fly. Conversational interaction allows user preferences to be clearly established: "more like this", "less like that", "none of those", etc.

Note that the distinction between the content-based recommender systems and the knowledge-based systems in publications on the subject is a very fine line. Many authors see content-based approaches as a subset of the knowledge-based approaches. However, in this book, we have chosen to use the classification established by [ADO 05], in which content-based approaches are characterized by the use of information contained in item characteristics (descriptions); in the case of the knowledge-based approaches, information and knowledge must be added in order to produce recommendations.

2.8. Hybrid approaches

Hybrid recommender systems make use of components or logic from different types of recommendation approaches (an overview is given in [BUR 02]). For example, a system of this type might use both external knowledge and item characteristics, combining collaborative filtering and content-based approaches.

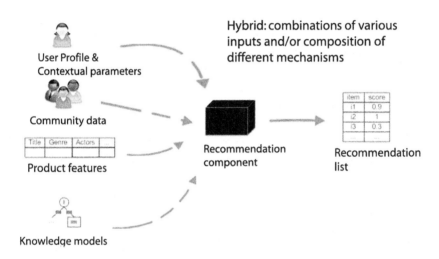

Figure 2.6. *Hybrid recommender system seen as a black box [JAN 10]*

Note that the notion of "hybrid" is an artifact of the historical evolution of recommender systems, in which certain types of knowledge sources were first used, producing well-established techniques; these techniques were later combined. If the notion of recommendation is considered as a problem for which the solution may be based on multiple knowledge sources, our sole concern is to identify which sources are most appropriate for a given task and to determine the most efficient way of using these sources. This process is shown in Figure 2.6.

There are three broad categories of system combinations used in designing hybrid recommender systems [BUR 02, JAN 10]: monolithic hybridization design, parallelized hybridization design and pipelined hybridization design.

The monolithic hybridization design integrates aspects of different recommendation strategies into a single algorithm. As shown in Figure 2.7, different recommender systems contribute to this process, as the hybrid approach uses additional input data that are specific to another recommendation algorithm; in other cases, input data may be supplemented using one technique and exploited using another technique. For example, an essentially content-based recommender system making use of community data to determine similarities between items would fall into this category.

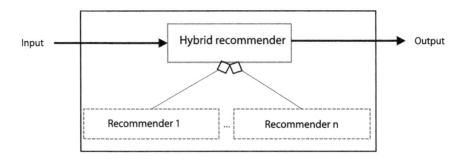

Figure 2.7. *Monolithic hybridization design [JAN 10]*

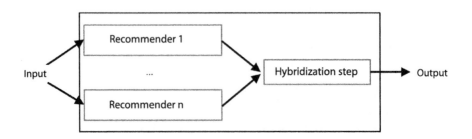

Figure 2.8. *Parallelized hybridization design [JAN 10]*

The two other hybridization approaches require at least two separate implementations of recommendation processes, which are then combined.

Parallelized hybrid recommender systems operate independently using the same input data and produce separate lists of recommendations, as shown in Figure 2.8.

These outputs are then combined in a later hybridization step in order to produce a final set of recommendations.

When several recommender systems are linked via a pipeline architecture, as shown in Figure 2.9, the output from one recommender system provides part of the input data for the following system. Initial input data may sometimes be used to supplement the input data for one or more of the systems in the pipeline.

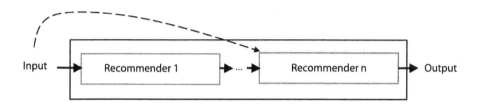

Figure 2.9. *Pipelined hybridization design [JAN 10]*

2.9. Other approaches

Other recommendation approaches also exist. Few examples include the following:

– graph-based recommender systems [RIC 11], similar to collaborative filtering approaches, in which data are represented in the form of a graph, where nodes are users, items or both, and edges are used to represent interactions or similarities between users and/or items. Figure 2.10 shows a representation of these approaches (based on Example 2.1 for scores ≥ 5) in which data are modeled in the form of a bipartite graph[5], where the two sets of nodes represent users and items, and an edge is placed between each user c and item i if i has been given a score by c;

---

5 In the graph theory, a graph is said to be "bipartite" if the set of vertices can be split into two subsets, U and V, so that each edge has one extremity in U and the other in V.

– trust-based or trust-aware recommender systems [AND 08, GOL 08, JAN 10, RIC 11] have emerged with the development of the Internet. Again, these systems are similar to collaborative filtering and are based on the sociological idea that users are more likely to have similar opinions and tastes to people they know and trust. Approaches of this type aim to refine classic recommendation techniques by exploiting trust relationships between the users within a network;

– context-aware recommender systems [ADO 08, JAN 10, RIC 11] adapt to the specific contextual situation of the user (location, people around him or her, available resources, etc.);

– group-based approaches may also be used as users rarely operate alone and rarely have only one requirement [RIC 11]. These approaches aggregate different information in order to best respond to the expectations of a group of users. Another variant takes the form of multicriteria approaches [ROY 96, LAK 11, RIC 11], which supply recommendations by modeling the utility of an item for a user as a score vector based on multiple criteria.

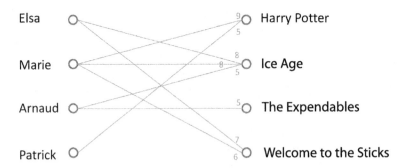

Figure 2.10. *Representation of scores as a bipartite graph*

This chapter has covered a number of different approaches used to propose recommendations to a user. The four most widespread approaches are content-based approaches, collaborative filtering approaches, knowledge-based approaches and hybrid approaches (a combination of other types of approach). Table 2.5 [6] *summarizes the advantages and disadvantages associated with each of these approaches (as hybrid approaches include a combination of other approaches, they possess the advantages and disadvantages of the component approaches).*

	Advantages	Disadvantages
Collaborative approaches	– Knowledge engineering is useless – Chance involved in results – Use of other users' scores	– Need for feedback – Cold start problem for new users and new items – Low density of *Users × Items* matrix – Data security issues
Content-based approaches	– Community data are useless – Possibility of comparing items – Comparison of user preferences with item characteristics – No cold start problem for new items – No issues with low matrix density	– Item descriptions required – Cold start problem for new users – Over-specialization – Need for feedback – Impossible to represent everything using keywords
Knowledge-based approaches	– Deterministic recommendations – Quality guaranteed – No cold start problem	– Need for knowledge engineering – Approaches are generally static – Recommendations are not particularly sensitive to short-term trends

Table 2.5. *Advantages and disadvantages of different recommendation approaches*

---

6 Recommendations are considered to be deterministic when the system always returns the same list of recommendations for the same user and the same catalog of items.

3

Key Concepts, Useful Measures and Techniques

Moins il y a de distance entre deux hommes, plus ils sont pointilleux pour le faire remarquer (The shorter the distance between two men, the greater their insistence that it should be noticed)
Antoine Rivarol, 1788

In this chapter, we consider ways in which similarity may be measured, including metrics and distances, alongside a number of other techniques used in the context of recommender systems. The approaches presented in the following sections are those discussed elsewhere in this book and correspond to defined contexts. This chapter does not aim to provide an exhaustive list of all existing methods but simply gives an overview of the most widely used methods in the context of recommender systems (see the previous chapter). Table 3.1 shows the contexts of use of the approaches discussed in the previous chapters. Note that many approaches may be used in a variety of contexts.

Similarity measures generally take the form of functions quantifying the relationship between two objects, compared on the basis of their similarities and differences. The two objects must, clearly, be of the same type. However, the value given for a measure of similarity between x and y may be different to that given between y and x. Thus, not all similarity measures are metrics. In mathematical terms, a metric, or a distance, is a value function within the set of real numbers $\mathbb{R}$, which defines the distance between the elements of a set X, such that $d : X \times X \to \mathbb{R}$.

	Data mining		Content-based approaches	Collaborative approaches		
	Preprocessing	Analysis		User-to-user	Item-to-item	Other
Euclidean distance	√					
Cosine similarity	√				√	
Pearson correlation	√			√		
PCA	√					√
SVD	√					√
kNN		√	√	√		
Decision trees		√	√			
Association rules		√				√
K-means		√				
Dice index			√			
TF-IDF			√			
LSA						√

Table 3.1. *Context of the approaches presented in this book*

Let x, y and z be three elements of a set, and let $d(x, y)$ be the distance between x and y. In order to be a metric, a measure d must satisfy the following four conditions:

– positivity: $d(x, y) \geq 0$;

– principle of identity of indiscernibles: $d(x, y) = 0 \equiv x = y$;

– symmetry: $d(x, y) = d(y, x)$;

– triangular inequality: $d(x, z) \leq d(x, y) + d(y, z)$.

These conditions express notions that are intuitive when considering the concept of distance, for example the fact that the distance between two distinct points must be positive and that the distance from x to y is the same as the distance from y to x. The triangular inequality means that the distance from x to z directly cannot be greater than that from x to y then from y to z.

In this chapter, we focus on syntactic approaches. A syntactic measure of similarity allows us, for example, to compare textual documents on the basis of the character sequences they contain: the sequences "truck" and "trucker" may be considered very similar, whereas "truck" and the British equivalent, "lorry", might be considered very different. This type of measure, applied to character sequences, produces a value that is obtained algorithmically.

3.1. Vector space model

Generally speaking, a user profile, community data and product characteristics may be represented using vectors. The representation of these different sets in vector form in a shared vector space is known as a vector space model.

In the context of recommender systems, items and users are, therefore, represented in vector form. In this case, we simplify the vector representation by limiting ourselves to vectors of size 4 (for reasons of readability and ease of calculation), showing keywords (in this case, relating to movie/book genres) shared by users and items. The value 1 will be used to indicate the presence of the keyword in an item's characteristics or in a user's profile, and the value of 0 will be used to indicate its absence.

EXAMPLE 3.1.– *On the basis of the profiles of Marie (see Table 2.1) and Arnaud (who likes the "Romance" and "Children's" genres) and our extract from a book catalog (see Table 2.2), we obtain the following vector representations:*

	Crime/thriller	Comedy	Children's	Romance
c_1: Marie	1	1	1	0
c_2: Arnaud	0	0	1	1
i_1: The Shining	1	0	0	0
i_2: Bridget Jones's Diary	0	1	0	1

This matrix will be used throughout this chapter.

3.2. Similarity measures

3.2.1. *Cosine similarity*

Cosine similarity [QAM 10] is often used [BAE 99] to measure similarity between documents. The cosine of the angle between the vector representations of items or users to be compared is calculated. The similarity obtained is expressed as $sim_{cosine} \in [0,1]$. In the case of two items i_1 and i_2, the formula is as follows:

$$sim_{cosine}(i_1, i_2) = \frac{\vec{i_1}.\vec{i_2}}{\|\vec{i_1}\|\|\vec{i_2}\|}$$

EXAMPLE 3.2.– *For items i_1 (The Shining) and i_2 (Bridget Jones's Diary), we thus have* $sim_{cosine} = (i_1, i_2) = \frac{\vec{i_1}.\vec{i_2}}{\|\vec{i_1}\|\|\vec{i_2}\|} = \frac{0}{\sqrt{1}.\sqrt{2}} = 0$ *showing that the two items have nothing in common. The two users c_1 and c_2 may be compared in the same way, giving $sim_{cosine}(c_1, c_2) \approx 0.408$; it is also possible to calculate the similarity between an item and a user, for example $sim_{cosine}(c_1, i_1) = 0.577$ and $sim_{cosine}(c_2, i_1) = 0$, which shows that item i_1 (The Shining) is more relevant for c_1 (Marie) than for c_2 (Arnaud).*

3.2.2. Pearson correlation coefficient

The Pearson correlation coefficient [ROD 88] calculates the similarity between two items or two users as the cosine of the angle between their standardized vector representation scores. The similarity obtained is expressed as $sim_{Pearson} \in [-1,1]$. For two users c_1 and c_2, the formula is as follows:

$$sim_{Pearson}(c_1, c_2) = sim_{cosine}(c_1 - \bar{c_1}, c_2 - \bar{c_2})$$

where $\bar{c_1}$ (resp. $\bar{c_2}$) represents the mean of c_1 (resp. c_2).

EXAMPLE 3.3.– *Retaining vectors of size 4, the mean for c_1, $\bar{c_1} = \frac{3}{4}$, for c_2, $\bar{c_2} = \frac{1}{2}$ and for i_1, $\bar{i_1} = \frac{1}{4}$, we obtain $sim_{Pearson}(c_1, c_2) = sim_{cosine}(c_1 - \bar{c_1}, c_2 - \bar{c_2}) = \frac{-1/2}{\sqrt{3/4}.\sqrt{1}} \approx -0.577$. In the same way, $sim_{Pearson}(c_1, i_1) \approx 0.333$ and $sim_{Pearson}(c_2, i_1) \approx -0.577$. This shows that, according to the Pearson correlation coefficient, item i_1 (The Shining) is more relevant for user c_1 (Marie).*

3.2.3. Euclidean distance

Euclidean distance is used to calculate the similarity between two items or users as the distance between their vector representations is reduced to a single point. In the case of two users c_1 and c_2, the formula is as follows:

$$sim_{Euclidean}(c_1,c_2) = \|\vec{c}_1 - \vec{c}_2\| = \sqrt{\sum\nolimits_{k=1}^{n} (c_{1_k} - c_{2_k})^2}$$

where n is the total number of represented terms, that is the size of the vectors.

EXAMPLE 3.4.– *Using vectors of size 4, we have* $sim_{Euclidean}(c_1,c_2) = \|\vec{c}_1 - \vec{c}_2\|$
$= \sqrt{\sum_{k=1}^{4}(c_{1_k} - c_{2_k})^2} = \sqrt{3} \approx 1.73$. *In the same way,* $sim_{Euclidean}(c_1, i_1) \approx 1.41$
and $sim_{Euclidean}(c_2, i_1) \approx 1.73$. *Hence, according to the Euclidean distance, i_1 is more relevant for c_1 than for c_2.*

3.2.4. Dice index

The Dice index [DIC 45] measures the similarity between two items or two users based on the number of common terms in the two vectors under consideration. In the case of two items i_1 and i_2, the formula is as follows:

$$sim_{Dice}(i_1,i_2) = \frac{2N_c(i_1,i_2)}{N_{i_1} + N_{i_2}}$$

where $N_c(i_1, i_2)$ is the number of terms shared by i_1 and i_2, and N_{i_1} (resp. N_{i_2}) is the number of terms of i_1 (resp. i_2).

EXAMPLE 3.5.– *Items i_1 and i_2 have no shared terms. Let us consider, as an example, that an item i_1 contains 36 words. A second item i_2 contains 21 words. Thus, the Dice index between the two items i_1 and i_2 is:*
$sim_{Dice}(i_1,i_2) = \dfrac{2N_c(i_1,i_2)}{N_{i_1} + N_{i_2}} = \dfrac{2*0}{36+21} = 0$. *In the same way, if* $N_{c_1} = 15$,
$sim_{Dice}(c_1, i_1) \approx 0.039$ *and if* $N_{c_1} = 5$, $sim_{Dice}(c_2, i_1) = 0$. *Consequently, according to the Dice index, i_1 is more relevant for c_1 than for c_2.*

3.3. Dimensionality reduction

In the context of recommender systems, where problems may be equated to an estimation of scores in a utility matrix (*Users* × *Items*), these matrices may contain very large numbers of users and/or items. This may be problematic during data exploration and analysis processes. In these cases, data processing tools are required to improve understanding of the value of the knowledge available from these data.

Dimensionality reduction is one of the oldest approaches used to respond to this problem. The aim of dimensionality reduction is to select or extract an optimal subset from the matrix, according to a predefined criterion. The selection of this subset allows us to eliminate information that is irrelevant or redundant with regard to the chosen criterion. This selection/extraction process thus reduces the dimension of the search space, making the data set more representative of the problem [FOD 02, GUÉ 06].

The main aims of dimensionality reduction are as follows:

– to make it easier to visualize and understand data;

– to reduce the required storage space;

– to reduce learning and use times;

– to identify relevant information.

3.3.1. *Principal component analysis*

Principal component analysis (PCA) [PEA 01, HUA 04] is a data analysis method used in multivariate statistics and consists of transforming correlated variables into new, decorrelated variables. These new variables are known as "principal components" or principal axes. As a dimensionality reduction technique, PCA allows us to reduce the number of variables used and to reduce redundancy levels in information sets (see [WIK 15b] for a detailed introduction). This approach involves both geometric and statistical aspects.

In mathematical terms, PCA constitutes a simple change of basis, moving from a representation of the initial data using a canonical basis[1] to a

---

1 In a matrix space with n lines and p columns, the canonical basis is the set of matrices $M_{i,j}$ presenting a value of 1 at the intersection between the ith line and the jth column, with 0 elsewhere.

representation on the basis of factors defined by the eigenvectors of the correlation matrix.

In more concrete terms, PCA is used to describe large data tables (e.g. the *Users* × *Items* utility matrix). In cases involving large numbers of users and/or items, simple graphical representation methods cannot be used to visualize the point cloud formed by the associated data. PCA helps representations to be produced in a space of lower dimensions, highlighting potential structures within data. This is achieved by focusing on subspaces in which the projection of the cloud deforms the initial cloud as little as possible.

3.3.2. Singular value decomposition

Singular value decomposition (SVD) [GOL 65] of a matrix is an important tool for factorizing real or complex rectangular matrices. It is a data reduction process [BAK 05].

In mathematical terms, let M be a matrix $n \times p$ (with n lines and p columns). SVD (see [JAN 10] for an example of SVD in the case of recommender systems for the *Users* × *Items* utility matrix) is a factorization algorithm that allows M to be expressed as the product of three specific matrices U, Σ and V such that:

$$M = U\Sigma V^T$$

with:

- U: orthogonal[2] matrix, $m \times m$;
- Σ: positive diagonal[3] matrix, $m \times n$;
- V^T: orthogonal matrix[4], $n \times n$.

---

2 A real square matrix A of order n is said to be orthogonal if it verifies one of the following equivalent properties:
- $^{T}AA = I_n$;
- $A^{T}A = I_n$;
- A is reversible and $A^{-1} = {^{T}A}$,
with I_n identity matrix of order n.
3 A positive diagonal matrix contains real numbers greater than or equal to zero along the diagonal, with all other cells containing values of zero.
4 The transposed matrix V^T of a matrix V is obtained by swapping lines and columns.

Note that, conventionally, values Σ_i are arranged in order of decreasing values of i. The Σ matrix is defined uniquely by M (unlike U and V).

3.3.3. *Latent semantic analysis*

Latent Semantic Analysis (LSA) or latent semantic indexation [DEE 90] is a process derived from natural language processing in the context of vector semantics. In this specific context, LSA may be used to establish relationships between a set of user profiles (resp. items) and the keywords they contain, by constructing "concepts" linked to users (resp. items) and to keywords. On the basis of the matrix that describes the frequency of certain keywords in user profiles (or item characteristics), which is a sparse matrix with lines corresponding to keywords[5] and columns corresponding to users (or items), LSA transforms this occurrence matrix into a relationship between keywords and "concepts", and a second relationship between these "concepts" and users (or items). It then allows us to obtain a lower-ranking matrix, giving an approximation of the occurrence matrix.

Intuitively, from the *Keyword* × *User* (resp. *Keyword* × *Item*) matrix, we see that the dimension of this matrix is reduced by applying, for example, an SVD to obtain a summary (unknown) consisting of "concepts". The initial matrix is then reconstructed, but using these reduced dimensions.

3.4. Classification/clustering

Classification/clustering involves grouping users or items using an organized and hierarchical categorization system.

3.4.1. *Classification*

The objective of classification is to define rules allowing users or items to be placed into classes based on characteristic qualitative or quantitative variables. A training sample with a known classification, that is a sample in which the classes used to divide users or items are known in advance, is used as a starting point. This sample is used for learning classification rules. Note

---

5 Keywords are generally words that have been truncated or reduced to a stem. The number of times a keyword appears in each profile is often standardized using the TF-IDF weighting.

that, by convention, a second independent test sample is used to validate this classification.

The most widely used classification methods and techniques include the following:

– *The k Nearest Neighbors (kNN) method* [COV 06]: this simple method consists of comparing a user/item of unknown class to all stored users/items. The majority class from the kNN is then selected. In more formal terms, using the users/items x' from the training sample and a new user/item x for classification, the process consists of:

- determining the k nearest users/items to x by calculating the distance between x and all x';

- counting the occurrences of each class for the k nearest users/items;

- assigning x to the most frequent class.

Note that this algorithm requires a defined value of k, the number of neighbors to consider, which may be determined by cross-validation. Similarly, the algorithm requires a distance between users/items, which may be obtained using different methods, such as those presented earlier in this chapter.

– *Decision trees* [QUI 86]: this is a graphical representation of a classification process, specifically in tree form, in which the "leaves" at the end of each branch represent different possible results in accordance with decisions made at each stage. In the context of recommendation, the nodes in the tree represent characteristics of items and are used to partition data, for example as a function of the presence or absence of a keyword in a profile. Figure 3.1 shows a decision tree in which two classes (*relevant* and *irrelevant*) are used to determine whether or not a new item is relevant.

3.4.2. *Clustering*

In classification, classes are known beforehand and the objective is to create a classification rule to predict the way in which new observations (users or items) will be classed. In clustering, however, clusters are not predetermined. The aim of clustering is to find a means of classifying observations (users or items) based on available descriptors (see [JAI 88] for further details).

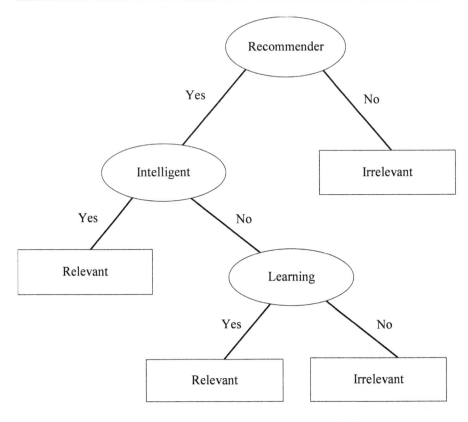

Figure 3.1. *Example of a decision tree [JAN 10]*

Clustering techniques include *K-means clustering* [HAR 79]: using this rapid algorithm, *K* distinct clusters are presumed to exist. The algorithm then uses *K* centers[6] of clusters $\mu_1, ..., \mu_K$ from users or items. The following steps are then carried out in an iterative manner:

1) for each user/item that is not a cluster center, the algorithm identifies the nearest cluster center, thus defining *K* clusters $P_1, ..., P_K$, where $P_j = \{$set *of points nearest the center* $\mu_j\}, \forall j \in [1, K]$;

2) in each new cluster P_j, the algorithm defines a new cluster center μ_j as the barycenter of the points of P_j.

---

6 These centers may be either selected because they are representative or designated at random.

The algorithm stops on reaching a determined STOP criterion: either the maximum number of iterations is reached, or the algorithm converges, that is the clusters remain identical from one iteration to the next, or the algorithm reaches a point of quasi-convergence, that is where intra-cluster inertia ceases to improve significantly from one iteration to the next.

3.5. Other techniques

Other techniques exist that do not fall into the categories of similarity measures, dimensionality reduction techniques and classification/clustering methods discussed earlier in the chapter. Two of these techniques are presented in sections 3.5.1 and 3.5.2.

3.5.1. *Term frequency-inverse document frequency (TF-IDF)*

In the context of recommender systems, TF-IDF is used to evaluate the importance of a term contained in a user profile or in the characteristics of an item, relative to a set of users or to a catalog of items. The weighting increases in proportion to the number of times the term occurs in a user's profile or in the characteristics of an item. It also varies as a function of the frequency of the term among all users or throughout the catalog. Thus, the inverse frequency of the user profile (resp. the item characteristic) (idf) measures the importance of the term in relation to the set of users (resp. the catalog).

In the case of TF-IDF, a higher weighting is given to the least frequent terms that are considered to be the most discriminating factors. This is carried out by calculating the logarithm of the inverse of the proportion of user profiles (or item characteristics) containing the term:

$$idf_k = log \frac{|C|}{\left|\{c_j : t_k \in c_j\}\right|} \text{ (resp. } idf_k = log \frac{|I|}{\left|\{i_j : t_k \in i_j\}\right|}\text{), where } |C| \text{ (resp. } |I|\text{)}$$

is the total number of users (profiles) (resp. total number of items) and $\left|\{c_j : t_k \in c_j\}\right|$ (resp. $\left|\{i_j : t_k \in i_j\}\right|$ is the number of profiles (resp. item characteristics) in which the term t_k appears. Finally, the weighting is obtained by multiplying the two measures: $tfidf_{k,j} = tf_{k,j}.idf_k$.

Note that the new vectors obtained using TF-IDF may be used as a basis for similarity measure calculations involving vector comparison (such as those discussed earlier).

EXAMPLE 3.6.– *Considering users (and continuing to use a maximum of four terms), our example contains two profiles (c_1 and c_2), thus $|C| = 2$. Only profile c_1 contains the term "Thriller/Crime". Consequently, $idf_{Thriller/Crime} = log\left(\frac{1}{2}\right) \approx 0.301$.*

In the same way, the term "Children's" appears in both profiles, so $idf_{Children's} = log\left(\frac{2}{2}\right) = 0$. The TF-IDF calculation for the term "Thriller/Crime" is therefore: $tfidf_{Thriller/Crime,c_1} = tf_{Thriller/Crime,c_1} \cdot idf_{Thriller/Crime} = \frac{1}{4}. log\frac{2}{1} \approx 0.075$ for profile c_1 and $tfidf_{Thriller/Crime,c_2} = tf_{Thriller/Crime,c_2} \cdot idf_{Thriller/Crime} = 0. log\frac{2}{1} = 0$ for profile c_2. For the term "Children's": $tfidf_{Children's,c_1} = tf_{Children's,c_1} \cdot idf_{Children's} = \frac{1}{4}. log\frac{2}{2} = 0$ for profile c_1 and $tfidf_{Children's,c_2} = tf_{Children's,c_2} \cdot idf_{Children's} = \frac{1}{4}. log\frac{2}{2} = 0$ for profile c_2.

The vector representations of c_1 and c_2 using TF-IDF are as follows:

	Thriller/Crime	Comedy	Children's	Romance
c_1	0.075	0.075	0	0
c_2	0	0	0	0.075

3.5.2. Association rules

An association rule [AGR 93, MAN 94] is an application of the form $X \Rightarrow Y$, where X and Y are disjoint sets of users/items, meaning that if X is "liked" then Y is also "liked". Note that an association rule shows co-occurrence, and not causality. These rules may be detected from the *Users × Items* utility matrix using special techniques.

The strength of an association rule may be measured by considering its support and confidence, for example:

$$Support(X \Rightarrow Y) = \frac{Number\ of\ transactions\ containing\ (U \cup X)}{Number\ of\ transactions}$$

$$Confidence(X \Rightarrow Y) = \frac{Number\ of\ transactions\ containing(U \cup X)}{Number\ of\ transactions\ containing\ X}$$

where a transaction is a subset of all users/items and describes a set of users/items that are scored together. In our specific context, using the *Users* × *Items* utility matrix, it is easy to consider a transaction for a set of items (resp. users) as a user (resp. an item) itself, that is a line (resp. column) in the matrix.

[LIN 02] proposed a formula to calculate the score of a user/item *e* based on these two measures:

$$score_e = \sum_{rules\ containing\ e} \left(Support(rule) * Confidence(rule) \right)$$

3.6. Comparisons

[HUA 08] and [STR 00], considering the performances of different measure techniques, showed that the performances of cosine similarity and the Pearson coefficient are very similar and significantly better than those obtained using Euclidean distance. However, [BAV 10] highlighted that the smaller the document, the better the result obtained using Euclidean distance; in these cases, the performance of cosine similarity is reduced.

	Advantages	Disadvantages
Vector model	– Whatever technique is used, vector-based approaches use the same initial format, i.e. vector representation – Techniques based on the vector model are easy to develop, requiring only vector calculations	– Identical words considered to be relevant can sometimes have too much influence on the similarity value. For example the term "the" in titles such as "The Godfather" and "The Little Mermaid" is not really relevant, but it will still have a certain weight – Note, however, that lemmatization, the elimination of "empty" words and TF-IDF can be used to counteract this effect
Syntactic approaches	– Techniques based on a syntactic approach leave no place for exceptions – This means they can be easily made automatic	– By definition, techniques based on the syntactic approach do not consider semantics. For example there is no obvious similarity between the terms "romantic" and "sentimental", despite the fact that the two words may be used to describe the same object

Table 3.2. *Advantages and disadvantages of the vector model and syntactic approaches*

It is also useful to list the main advantages and disadvantages of each type of approach, rather than each measure. The measures and techniques presented in this chapter are mostly based on the vector model, or fall into the category of syntactic approaches. The advantages and disadvantages of these two broad groups are presented in Table 3.2.

In conclusion, in this chapter, we discussed different techniques used in the context of recommender systems, whether in measuring the similarity between users, between items, or between users and items (cosine similarity, Pearson correlation coefficients, Euclidean distance and the Dice index), or in reducing the number of dimensions in order to make it easier to analyze relationships between users, items or users and items (PCA, SVD, LSA). A third group of techniques involves classifying or clustering users or items, and still other techniques may be used (TF-IDF, association rules). Note that each of these techniques has its own characteristics and may be used as a complement to any of the others.

4

Practical Implementations

> *It is easy to know something, but difficult to put that knowledge into practice*
> Chinese proverb

The different recommendation techniques presented in Chapter 2 are used in a variety of contexts, including commercial, industrial and academic applications. This chapter presents a number of ways in which these techniques are implemented in practice.

4.1. Commercial applications

Many systems that we use on a daily basis offer recommendations to their users: for example groups, jobs and people may be recommended by LinkedIn [LIN 15]; Facebook [FAC 15] recommends friends; systems such as Last.fm [LAS 15] recommend music, and Websites such as Forbes.com [FOR 15] recommend news stories. In this section, we describe the recommendation techniques used by Amazon.com [AMA 15] (for product recommendations) and by Netflix [NET 15] (for movie recommendations).

4.1.1. *Amazon.com*

Recommender systems are widely used by online retailers. Websites such as Amazon.com [AMA 15] (or other similar online retailers) present users with suggestions of products that they may wish to buy.

Recommendation algorithms are widely known due to their use by e-commerce sites, where client interests are used as input in order to generate lists of recommended products. Many applications only use details of products that clients have purchased and evaluated explicitly in order to represent these interests, but other attributes may also be included, such as lists of consulted products, demographic data and favorite artists. Amazon.com uses recommendation algorithms to personalize the online store for each client. The store changes radically in response to client interests, displaying programming products to software engineers, for example, and baby toys to young mothers.

The algorithm used by Amazon.com is based on item-based (or item-to-item) collaborative filtering. The online calculations used by the algorithm are independent of the number of clients and the number of products in the catalog. The algorithm offers recommendation in real time and is suitable for use with huge quantities of data [LIN 03].

Amazon.com uses recommendations as a targeted marketing tool. By clicking on the "Your Amazon" link, users are taken to an area in which they may filter recommendations by product type and/or category, evaluate product recommendations, evaluate previous purchases and understand why certain products have been recommended to them (see Figure 4.1). Moreover, as we see from Figure 4.2, the recommendation list in the cart suggests products to clients based on the contents of their cart. This function operates in a similar way to impulse purchases at the checkout line in a supermarket, except that in the case of Amazon.com, these suggested "impulse buys" are targeted at individual clients. Amazon.com uses recommendation algorithms to personalize its Website based on each client's specific interests.

Rather than matching user profiles with similar clients, item-to-item collaborative filtering matches each product purchased and/or evaluated by a client with similar products, then combines these similar products into a list of recommendations. To determine which matches are most similar to a given product, the algorithm constructs a matrix of similar products, aiming to identify products that clients often purchase together. Given a matrix of similar products, the algorithm identifies products that are similar to each item purchased and/or evaluated by the user, aggregates the products and then recommends the most popular or most closely correlated articles. This calculation is extremely rapid, as it depends only on the number of products purchased and/or evaluated by the user.

The Nightingale
Kristin Hannah
☆☆☆☆☆(382) $11.89
Fix this recommendation

Go Set a Watchman: A
Novel
Harper Lee
☆☆☆☆☆(715) $16.07
Fix this recommendation

Figure 4.1. *"Your Amazon" on Amazon.com*

Your Recently Viewed Items and Featured Recommendations

Inspired by your browsing history   Page 1 of 9

Doctor Sleep	Dark Places	Full Dark, No Stars	Under the Dome: A Novel
› Stephen King	› Gillian Flynn	› Stephen King	› Stephen King
★★★★☆ 8,473	★★★★★ 7,192	★★★★☆ 1,325	★★★★☆ 5,063
Paperback	Paperback	Mass Market Paperback	Paperback
$9.54 √Prime	$8.33 √Prime	$7.49 √Prime	$14.47 √Prime

Figure 4.2. *In-cart recommendations on Amazon.com*

4.1.2. Netflix

Netflix [NET 15] is an online movie rental service that allows users to rent movies for a monthly fee, based on a list of movies that they wish to see in a given order of priority. Movies are then sent out to users or delivered via streaming. Using the DVD option, users simply mail the disk back to the company, and the next movie is mailed out, with no carriage charges.

The length of time subscribers stay with the service is linked to the number of movies they watch and enjoy. If users are unable to find movies that they wish to watch, they will tend to leave the service. A successful recommendation service is therefore essential, both for the company and for the subscribers, to guarantee that users will find movies that they love. The company encourages subscribers to evaluate the movies they watch. Currently, Netflix holds over 1.9 billion evaluations, given by more than 11.7 million subscribers to more than 85,000 titles since October 1998. The company has delivered more than 1 billion DVDs and mails out more than 1.5 million DVDs each day. The service receives more than 2 million evaluations each day.

The hybrid recommender system used by Netflix, known as Cinematch, analyzes the cumulated scores of movies and uses these scores to make hundreds of millions of personalized predictions for users on a daily basis, taking account of personal tastes. The Cinematch system automatically analyzes the cumulated scores of movies on a weekly schedule, using a variation on the Pearson correlation coefficient with all other movies in order to construct a list of "similar" movies that are likely to appeal to the same users. As users provide scores, the online, real-time aspect of the system uses these scores to calculate a multivariate regression[1] based on these correlations in order to create a unique, personalized prediction for each recommendable movie. If no personalized recommendations are available, the average score given to movies is used. These predictions are shown on the Website using red stars [BEN 07].

For Netflix, the question of precise score prediction is so important that, since 2006, certain prizes have been offered to developers, such as a 1 million dollar payout for the first algorithm to perform 10% better[2] than the Netflix recommender system of the time. The prize was won in 2009 by a research team known as BellKor's Pragmatic Chaos [KOR 09], more than 3 years after the competition was launched.

4.2. Databases

Considerable attention has been given to recommender systems in the context of databases (a well-known and widely used data structuring method). In e-commerce, a recommendation is the item $i \in I$ (the set of all

1 Multiple linear regression is a statistical analysis technique that describes variations in an endogenous variable associated with variations in several exogenous variables.

2 More precisely, the algorithm had to have a Root Mean Square Error (RMSE) 10% lower than that of the Netflix algorithm, for a test set taken from real Netflix user scores. For development purposes, participants were given a data sample (also using real Netflix data). The winners of Netflix prizes are required to document and publish their approaches, enabling anyone to understand and benefit from the techniques and knowledge available to produce the best possible results.

items (movies, books, etc.)) with the maximum utility value for a user $c \in C$ (set of all users). By analogy, a recommendation in the context of databases is defined as a query such that the utility for a query session[3] $s \in S$ (set of all possible sessions) is maximized.

DEFINITION 4.1.– *Recommendation in databases.*

Let Q_T be the set of all possible queries for a database[4], and S the set of all possible sessions using the database, given a log of query sessions, a database and a current session, and let u be a function measuring the utility of a query q for a session s, that is $u : S \times Q_T \to \mathbb{R}$. Thus, for each query session $s \in S$, the recommended query $q' \in Q_T$ is that which maximizes the utility for the session: $\forall s \in S, q'_s = argmax_{q \in Q_T} u(s,q).$

EXAMPLE 4.1.– *In this example, we consider query sessions launched by different users.*

We obtain a matrix $S \times Q_T$:

$u(s, q)$	q_1	q_2	q_2^2	q_3	q_3^2	q_4	q_5	q_6
s_1	3		5		9			
s_2	2			5	5	8		
s_3	2		5				6	9
s_c	2	3		5				

Note that each cell (s, q) of the matrix corresponds to the utility score assigned to query q for session s.

In the context of databases, many authors [CHA 09, KHO 09, STE 09] have proposed methods and algorithms to assist users in the construction of queries. In the specific case of recommendations for data warehouses (often seen as the "heart" of a decision support system) using online analytical process (OLAP) queries (see [MAR 11] and [NEG 09] for further details), some authors use the profiles and preferences of decision-makers [BEL 05, JER 09, GOL 11], whereas others rely on knowledge discovery through decision analysis [SAR 00, CAR 08]. Other approaches are based on the use

---

3 A query is a command responding to a specific syntax allowing information handling within a database.
4 In practice, as in the case of e-commerce, we consider a finite subset of this set.

of logs containing previous query sequences for other users involving the same data cube[5] [SAP 99, CHA 09, GIA 09, YAN 09, GIA 11].

4.3. Collaborative environments

Collaboration may be defined as a shared process in which two or more individuals, with complementary abilities, interact in order to create shared understanding [SCH 90]. This collaboration may be facilitated by the use of a computer-based environment; the E-MEMORAe2.0 Web platform serves this objective [ABE 09]. Environments of this type can also make use of interaction traces. In this context, a trace is defined by [ZAR 11] as a record of the actions carried out by a user using a system. A number of projects are currently underway concerning the use of these traces for various purposes, including decision support and recommendation.

Many authors have also considered ways of exploiting interaction traces [DJO 08]. [LI 13] distinguished between four types of traces (private, collaborative, collective, personal):

– a private trace, which is emitted and received by the same user;

– a collaborative trace, which has a single emitter and several receivers;

– a collective trace, which has several emitters and several receivers;

– a personal trace, which has a single emitter, but with no limitations as to the number of receivers.

This model allows us to obtain a more detailed analysis of user interactions. It notably highlights exchanges between members using a computing environment. One of the main uses of these traces is in the field of recommender systems. The utility of traces for recommender systems is further shown by the quantity of information requiring processing and the need for assistance in reducing the workload [ADO 05].

[WAN 14] and [WAN 15] have considered the use of semantic models in exploiting interaction traces for recommendation purposes. The authors chose to use the trace model typology defined by [LI 13] to establish

5 A data cube is a multidimensional representation of data used by decision-makers to explore data and implement OLAP analyses.

ad hoc recommendations[6]. They distinguished between different types of recommendations:

– group recommendations (to improve collaboration, identify risks, identify opportunities, etc., for a set of users working as a group);

– individual recommendations (to improve efficiency and individual organization in the accomplishment of different tasks);

– private recommendations (to improve a user's personal organization);

– collective recommendations (to improve communications within an organization, etc.).

The recommender system that the authors aim to create also considered a semantic model (who is working on what, and with whom; subject A is closest to subject B, etc.) and recorded interaction traces (who has shared documents, on what subjects, and with whom; who is frequently in contact with a given expert; etc.).

4.4. Smart cities

The concept of "smart cities" has yet to be clearly defined. However, six characteristics or categories are used when classifying and comparing this type of city: smart economy, smart mobility, smart environment, smart people, smart living and smart governance. Achievement of this "smart" quality is an increasingly important challenge for many cities or communities. It is particularly important in the context of ICT and for systems involving economic, social and other issues.

It is therefore important to assist cities in improving their "smartness" level. This area of recommendation is an emerging domain that shows great promise.

Recommender systems usually aim to predict the "score" that a user will give to an item (music, books, etc.), as yet unseen, using a model constructed based on the characteristics of certain items (in the case of content-based approaches) or the user's social environment (in the case of collaborative filtering approaches).

---

6 An *ad hoc* recommendation is a recommendation created specially in response to a specific need.

[NEG 14] presented a framework for a recommender system for cities. The aim of this research project was to identify the strengths of cities that have been recognized as "smart" and to apply the same actions to other cities with the same aims. The method comprised using a list of characteristics of a "smart" city and a list of characteristics of a city aiming to become "smart" to identify the actions needed for these aims to be achieved, based on given "smart" characteristics.

The key idea behind this method was the recommendation of actions that have already been implemented in "smart" cities with similar characteristics (the similarity of two cities is based on indicators such as air quality and water consumption) and actions that need to be implemented in this city.

Using an analogy from the field of e-commerce, a recommendation for "smart cities" may be defined as an action $a \in A$ (set of all possible actions) to implement, such that the utility for a city $v \in V$ (set of all possible cities) is maximized.

DEFINITION 4.2.– *Recommendation for "smart cities".*

Let A be the set of all possible actions and V the set of all cities, given a log of cities and a specific city that aims to become "smarter", and let u be a function measuring the utility[7] of an action a for a city v, that is $u : A \times V \rightarrow \mathbb{R}$. Hence, for each city $v \in V$, the recommended action $a' \in A$ is that which has the maximum utility value for the city:
$$\forall v \in V, a'_v = argmax_{a \in A} u(v, a).$$

EXAMPLE 4.2.– *Generally speaking, it is possible to create a matrix $V \times A$ in which a score indicates whether an action has been implemented and whether the implementing city considered this action to be effective:*

$u(v,a)$	Action 1	Action 2	Action 3	Action 4	Action 5
City 1	8	7			
City 2	9		3		
City 3	3	5		5	5
City 4	5	3		3	3

---

7 Scores are attributed by a person with the authority to implement different actions, who indicates, through this score, whether or not an action is (or was) relevant.

Note that each cell (v, a) in this matrix corresponds to the utility score assigned to action a for city v. Examples of actions may include "switch off street lighting after midnight". Finally, note that scores are given overall, but these overall scores may be obtained by combining notions of the cost and time involved in implementing the action, etc.

EXAMPLE 4.3.– *This example provides a more concrete illustration of action recommendations for smart cities (using hypothetical data). We shall use a log containing information concerning two fictional cities: Smallville and Metropolis. An extract from the log is as follows:*

Smallville= ⟨Small city in the USA, {smart environment, {sustainable development, {⟨water consumption, 300 (liters per year), {stop public fountains after midnight, do not water plants in summer}⟩, ⟨electricity consumption, 3000 (kW per year), {switch off public lighting after midnight, install solar street lighting}⟩}, pollution, {⟨air quality, $\frac{10}{10}$, Ø ⟩ }}}⟩

Metropolis= ⟨Large city in the USA, {smart environment, {sustainable development, {⟨water consumption, 100 000 (liters per year), {stop public fountains after midnight, do not wash cars in summer}⟩, ⟨electricity consumption, 200 000 (kW per year), {switch off public lighting after midnight}⟩}, pollution, {⟨air quality, $\frac{8}{10}$, {restrict downtown vehicle access, reduce vehicle speeds on main routes }⟩}}}⟩

Now suppose that a third city, Gotham, wishes to become more "smart" in the smart environment category, where:

Gotham= ⟨Batman's city, {smart environment, {sustainable development, {⟨water consumption, 150 000 (liters per year), Ø ⟩, ⟨electricity consumption, 100 000 (kW per year), {switch off public lighting after midnight}⟩}, pollution, {⟨air quality, $\frac{8}{10}$, Ø ⟩}}}⟩.

Table 4.1 summarizes the information available for each city.

	Smart environment					
	Sustainable development				Pollution	
	Water consumption		Electricity consumption		Air quality	
	Value (liters per year)	Actions	Value (kW per year)	Actions	Value (ratio)	Actions
Smallville	300	– Stop public fountains after midnight – Do not water plants in summer	3,000	– Switch off public lighting after midnight – Install solar street lighting	$\frac{10}{10}$	Ø
Metropolis	100,000	– Stop public fountains after midnight – Do not wash cars in summer	200,000	– Switch off public lighting after midnight	$\frac{8}{10}$	– Restrict downtown vehicle access – Reduce vehicle speeds on main routes
Gotham	150,000	Ø	100,000	– Switch off public lighting after midnight	$\frac{8}{10}$	Ø

Table 4.1. *Values for cities Smallville, Metropolis and Gotham*

The corresponding utility matrix might be:

$u(v, a)$	A_1	A_2	A_3	A_4	A_5	A_6	A_7
Smallville	9	7		8	8		
Metropolis	8		6	7		5	5
Gotham				8			

where action A_1 is *"stop public fountains after midnight"*, A_2 is *"do not water plants in summer"*, A_3 is *"do not wash cars in summer"*, A_4 is *"switch off public lighting after midnight"*, A_5 is *"install solar street lighting"*, A_6 is *"restrict downtown vehicle access" and A_7 is "reduce vehicle speeds on main routes".*

Information for the Smart environment category is available from the logs for Smallville and Metropolis. These two cities may be used to assist Gotham in making improvements in this category.

We shall therefore consider that the indicator values for Smallville and Metroplis are good values in terms of "smartness".

This category includes two key factors: sustainable development and pollution. The sustainable development factor includes two indicators: water consumption and electricity consumption. The available water consumption values are 100,000 for Metropolis and 300 for Smallville, giving a corresponding value interval of [300; 100,000]. The available electricity consumption values are 200,000 for Metropolis and 3,000 for Smallville, giving a corresponding value interval of [3,000; 200,000]. The pollution factor is determined by a single factor, air quality, with values of $\frac{8}{10}$ for Metropolis and $\frac{10}{10}$ for Smallville. The corresponding value interval is thus $\left[\frac{8}{10}, \frac{10}{10} \right]$.

Table 4.2 shows the intervals and values available for Gotham.

	Smart environment		
	Sustainable development		Pollution
	Water consumption	Electricity consumption	Air quality
Intervals	[300; 100,000]	[3,000; 200,000]	$\left[\frac{8}{10}, \frac{10}{10} \right]$
Gotham	150,000	100,000	$\frac{8}{10}$

Table 4.2. *Value intervals for Gotham*

The set of actions (implemented in the cities covered by the log: Smallville and Metropolis) that may be recommended to Gotham in order to improve "smartness" corresponds to the indicators for which the values for Gotham lie outside of the established intervals. Here (see Table 4.2), the water consumption value for Gotham is the only value that lies outside of these limits. Actions that may therefore be useful are those already implemented by Smallville and Metropolis for the water consumption indicator, including "do not wash vehicles in summer", "do not water plants in summer" and "stop public fountains after midnight".

These actions then need to be arranged by order of priority, for example according to ease of implementation. It is much easier to arrange for the water supply to public fountains to be stopped after midnight than to prevent a population from using water to wash their cars in the summer. Thus, a prioritized list of actions to implement for Gotham to improve environmental "smartness" might be: (1) "stop public fountains after midnight", (2) "do not water plants in summer" and (3) "do not wash vehicles in summer".

The corresponding utility matrix might be:

$u(v, a)$	A_1	A_2	A_3	A_4	A_5	A_6	A_7
Smallville	9	7		8	8		
Metropolis	8		6	7		5	5
Gotham	9	7	6	8			

4.5. Early warning systems

An early warning system can be defined as "a chain of information communication systems comprising sensor, detection, decision and broker subsystems, in the given order, working in conjunction, forecasting and signaling disturbances adversely affecting the stability of the physical world; and giving sufficient time for the response system to prepare resources and response actions to minimize the impact on the stability of the physical world" [WAI 10].

[NEG 13] presented a framework for recommender systems for crisis management. This framework uses previously implemented actions to improve the management of later crises, based on the central idea of using actions implemented for previous, similar crises (similarity is based on indicators such as time interval and type (hurricane, tsunami, etc.)) as recommendations. Finally, [NEG 13] suggested using knowledge acquired from past experience to improve future decisions (i.e. optimal action identification) regarding the management of imminent crises.

To use an analogy with e-commerce, a recommendation for early warning is defined as an action $a \in A$ (set of all possible actions) to implement in order to maximize utility in relation to a warning $w \in W$ (set of all possible warnings).

DEFINITION 4.3.– *Recommendation for early warnings.*

Let A be the set of all possible actions and W the set of all warnings, given a warning log, corresponding indicators and a current triggered warning, and let u be a function that measures the utility of an action a for a warning w, that is $u : W \times A \rightarrow \mathbb{R}$. Hence, for each warning $w \in W$, the recommended action $a' \in A$ is that which maximizes the utility for the warning:
$$\forall w \in W, a'_w = argmax_{a \in A} u(w, a).$$

EXAMPLE 4.4.– *This example provides a simple illustration of the obtained matrix $W \times A$ in which each score indicates that an action has been implemented and whether or not the action was considered to be effective:*

u(w, a)	Action 1	Action 2	Action 3	Action 4	Action 5
Warning 1	8	7			
Warning 2	9		3		
Warning 3	3	5		5	5
Warning 4	5	3		3	3

Note that each cell (w, a) in the matrix corresponds to the utility score assigned to action a for warning w.

In conclusion, this chapter has shown how the different recommendation techniques presented in Chapter 2 are implemented in practice (for commercial, industrial, academic and other applications) in a variety of domains, including Internet technologies, databases, collaborative working environments, smart cities and early warning systems.

5

Evaluating the Quality of Recommender Systems

Il y a de méchantes qualités qui font de grands talents (Some bad qualities form
great talents)
François de La Rochefoucauld, *Maxims*, 1665

In the previous chapters, we introduced different recommendation techniques and a certain number of systems. These techniques and systems evolve over time, attempting to move ever closer to the expectations and requirements of users. This process requires us to evaluate recommender systems in order to verify whether or not they are relevant and offer the required levels of performance for users in relation to context, objectives, response time, consideration of certain criteria, etc.

5.1. Data sets, sparsity and errors

In the context of recommender systems, consideration is given to specific groups within a population (online customers, Internet users, etc.) to propose or suggest suitable, personalized items. To do this, a set of data is required, whether synthetic or, better, "historic" records of user interactions with a system, that is a collection of user profiles with preferences, scores, transactions, etc. The use of a single data set to evaluate different recommender systems makes it easier to compare the performance of these different systems directly.

However, due consideration must be given to the density of the data set, which corresponds to the relationship between empty and full cells of the *Users × Items* matrix:

$$sparsity = 1 - \frac{|R|}{|I|.|C|}$$

where R is the set of scores, I is the set of items and C is the set of users making up the data set. Note that the sparsity value falls within the interval [0,1], where a value close to 0 indicates high density and a value close to 1 indicates low density in the data set.

A large number of public data sets are available, some of which are presented in Table 5.1.

Data set	Domain	Number of users	Number of items	Number of scores	Density
MovieLens 100k	Movies	967	4,700	100,000	0.978
MovieLens 1M	Movies	6,040	3,900	1 million	0.9575
MovieLens 10M	Movies	71,567	10,681	10 million	0.9869
Netflix	Movies	480,000	18,000	100 million	0.9999
Jester	Jokes	73,421	101	4.1 million	0.4471

Table 5.1. *Data sets*

However, the evaluation results of a recommender system using historical data sets cannot truly be compared to studies carried out using real users. As we see from Table 5.2:

– if the recommended item is truly relevant for the user, then the prediction was correct;

– if the recommended item is not indicated as being relevant for the user, this may be a false positive, where the system proposes an item not indicated as relevant in the history; however, this may be because the user was not aware of this item and might have found it to be relevant had he or she been aware of its existence;

– similarly, if an item is not recommended, then it is difficult to determine whether or not a user would have considered this unproposed item to be relevant; in this case, we have a false negative;

– if an item is not recommended and was not indicated as being relevant for the user, then the omission was correct.

		Item proposed by the recommender system	
		Yes	No
Item liked	Yes	Correct predictions	False negatives
by user	No	False positives	Correct omissions

Table 5.2. *Types of error [JAN 10]*

5.2. Measures

The quality of recommender systems may be measured in many ways. The most widespread notion is that of accuracy (see [HER 04] for further details). In this section, we focus on the best-known measures used in evaluating recommender systems using data sets.

5.2.1. *Accuracy*

Three types of accuracy may be considered: accuracy in predicting recommendations, accuracy in classifying recommendations and accuracy in ranking recommendations.

5.2.1.1. *Prediction accuracy*

The accuracy of predictions allows us to evaluate the capacity of a recommender system to correctly predict a user's opinion of a given item.

The most commonly used measures, taken from the field of statistics, are Mean Absolute Error (MAE) and Root-Mean-Square Error (RMSE). In the context of recommender systems, these values are used to measure the difference between predicted recommendation scores $reco(c, i)$ and real scores $r_{c,i}$ for all users $c \in C$ and all tested items $i \in Itest_c$.

MAE calculates the standard deviation between predicted and real scores, such that:

$$MAE = \frac{\sum_{c \in C} \sum_{i \in Itest_c} |reco(c,i) - r_{c,i}|}{\sum_{c \in C} |Itest_c|}$$

RMSE is the square root of the arithmetic mean of the squared errors between predicted and real scores, that is the mean size of the error. This measure is similar to MAE but highlights the widest deviations by giving a higher weighting to larger errors:

$$RMSE = \sqrt{\frac{\sum_{c \in C} \sum_{i \in Itest_c} (reco(c,i) - r_{c,i})^2}{\sum_{c \in C} Itest_c}}$$

The values of MAE and RMSE are situated in the interval $[0, +\infty)$ and are negative-oriented, that is the lower the value, the better the results. These results may be normalized[1] in order to make results easier to interpret. This gives new normalized forms of MAE and RMSE, known as NMAE and NRMSE, such that:

$$NMAE = \frac{MAE}{r_{max} - r_{min}} \quad \text{and} \quad NRMSE = \frac{RMSE}{r_{max} - r_{min}}$$

where r_{max} and r_{min} are the highest and lowest existing scores in $Itest_c$.

5.2.1.2. Classification accuracy

In the context of recommender systems, the aim of classification processes is to identify the most relevant items for a given user. The two most widespread measures are precision and recall (developed in the context of information retrieval [BAE 99]).

Precision, $Precision_c$, calculates the number of successes for a user c, $success_c$, that is the number of relevant items correctly recommended for user c, in relation to the total number of items recommended for the same

---

1 A measure is considered normalized when its values are found in the interval of values in $\mathbb{R}$, [0, 1].

user c. Users want proposed items to correspond to their requirements, and all irrelevant recommended items constitute noise. This noise is the opposite of precision; with high levels of precision, the system recommends few irrelevant items and may be considered to be "precise". Precision may be defined as follows:

$$Precision_c = \frac{Number\ of\ successes\ for\ c}{Total\ number\ of\ items\ recommended\ to\ c}$$

Recall, $Recall_c$, on the other hand, calculates the relationship between the number of successes for c, $successes_c$, and the theoretical maximum number of successes, $successes_T$, with regard to the size of the test set. Recall is defined by the number of relevant items recommended as a function of the number of relevant items in the test set. Users wish to see all items that may potentially respond to their preferences. If there is a high match rate between user preferences and the number of recommended items, then the recall rate is high. Conversely, if a high number of interesting items are present in the test set but do not appear in the recommendation list, the system is said to be "silent", showing a low recall rate. Recall may be defined as follows:

$$Recall_c = \frac{Number\ of\ successes\ for\ c}{Total\ number\ of\ existing\ relevant\ items} = \frac{|successes_c|}{|successes_T|}$$

A perfect recommender system would produce precision and recall values of 1 (that is the algorithm finds all relevant items – recall – and makes no errors – precision). However, algorithms may be more or less precise, and more or less relevant. Systems may often present high levels of precision, but with poor performance (precision $\approx$ 0.99, recall $\approx$ 0.10), or poor precision with high performance (precision $\approx$ 0.10, recall $\approx$ 0.99). For this reason, it is generally better to use the F_1-measure that combines precision and recall:

$$F_{1_c} = \frac{2 \cdot (Precision_c \cdot Recall_c)}{(Precision_c + Recall_c)}$$

5.2.1.3. *Ranking accuracy*

Measures of ranking accuracy build on the results of classification precision measures, taking account of the relative positions of successful recommendations in the list. In this section, we consider the most widespread techniques for measuring ranking accuracy: the Rank score [BRE 98], the Lift index [LIN 98], and the Discounted Cumulative Gain (DCG) [MAN 08].

The Rank score or R-score [BRE 98] builds on the notion of the recall measure, taking account of the positions of correct items in an ordered list (this is important in recommender systems, as items at the bottom of a list may be ignored by users). The Rank score is defined as the relationship between the score of correct items and the best theoretically attainable score:

$$RankScore = 100 \frac{\sum_c RankScore_c}{\sum_c RankScore_c^{max}}$$

where $RankScore_c = \sum_{i \in successes_c} \frac{max(r_{c,i} - d;0)}{2^{\frac{rank(i)-1}{\alpha-1}}}$, where d corresponds to a neutral vote and α corresponds to the item rank in the list, such that there are equal chances that the user will consider the item; and $RankScore_c^{max}$ is the maximum achievable score if all items recommended to user c were in first position in the recommendation list (ordered by vote value).

Note that [JAN 10] proposed a definition of $RankScore_c^{max} = \sum_{i=1}^{|ITest_c|} \frac{1}{2^{\frac{i-1}{\alpha}}}$.

The Lift index [LIN 98] divides the ordered recommendation list into 10 equal deciles[2] D_k and counts the number of successes for a user c in each decile, with $\sum_{k=1}^{10} D_k = |successes_c|$, such that:

---

2 In descriptive statistics, a decile is any of the 9 values that divide the sorted data into 10 equal parts, so that each part represents 1/10 of the sample or population. In the case of ordered recommendations, the deciles are values that divide the set of recommendations into 10 equal parts, so that the first decile corresponds to the score below which 10% scores are situated, whereas 90% scores are situated below the ninth decile.

$$liftIndex_c = \begin{cases} \dfrac{1.D_{1,c} + 0,9.D_{2,c} + ... + 0,1.D_{10,c}}{\sum_{k=1}^{10} D_{k,c}} & if \left| successes_c \right| > 0 \\ 0 & otherwise \end{cases}$$

Note that the Lift index gives an even lower weighting than the Rank score to successes situated at the top of the list.

Using DCG [MAN 08], positions are reduced logarithmically. Supposing that each user c has a "gain" (usefulness) value $g(c,i)$ for a recommended item i, DCG for a list of items $ITest_c$ is defined as follows:

$$DCG_c = \sum_{i=1}^{|ITest_c|} \frac{g(c,i)}{max(1, \log_b(i))}$$

where the base of logarithm b is a free parameter (traditionally between 2 and 10). Generally speaking, base 2 is used. A normalized version of this measure also exists, *NDCG* [JÄR 02].

Note that, according to [JAN 10], there is a relationship between the three ranking accuracy results discussed earlier, such that: *Rankscore < LiftIndex < DCG*. This relationship is because the Rank score is based on an exponential reduction, the Lift index on a linear reduction and DCG on a logarithmic reduction.

5.2.2. Other measures

Clearly, a wide variety of different measures may be used to quantify the quality of recommender systems, and not all of these techniques have been presented here. In addition to accuracy, measures may also be based on considerations such as:

– user coverage [ASS 14], when large numbers of users C use the system and the behavior of the recommender system in relation to new users with few scores needs to be verified, for example:

$$U_{cov} = \frac{\sum_{c \in C} \rho_c}{|C|} \quad where \; \rho_c = \begin{cases} 1 & if \; the \; number \; of \; recommendations > 0 \\ 0 & otherwise \end{cases}$$

– recommendation diversity, for example using Intra-List Similarity (ILS) [ZIE 05], which calculates the similarity between recommended items two by two; the lower the ILS value, the higher the diversity of recommended items.

In conclusion, in this chapter, we have presented different techniques used to evaluate the quality of recommender systems. Using data sets of varying sparsity (preferably made up of "historical" data), it is possible to measure prediction accuracy (MAE, RMSE, NMAE), classification accuracy (Precision, Recall, F_1-measure), ranking accuracy (Rank score, Lift index, DCG), user coverage (U_{cov}) or recommendation diversity (ILS). Note that each of these techniques has its own characteristics and may be used as a complement to any of the others.

Conclusion

This book provides an introduction to recommender systems. In the context of ever-increasing amounts of available information and data, it is difficult to know what information to look for and where to look for it. Computer-based techniques have been developed to facilitate the search and retrieval process; one of these techniques is recommendation, which guides users in their exploration of available information by seeking and highlighting the most relevant information.

Recommender systems have their origins in a variety of areas of research, including information retrieval, information filtering, text classification, etc. They use techniques such as machine learning and data mining, alongside a range of concepts including algorithms, collaborative and hybrid approaches, and evaluation methods.

Having first presented the notions inherent in data and information-handling systems (information systems, decision support systems and recommender systems) and established a clear distinction between recommendation and personalization, we then presented the most widespread approaches used in producing recommendations for users (content-based approaches, collaborative filtering approaches, knowledge-based approaches and hybrid approaches), alongside different techniques used in the context of recommender systems (user/item similarity, user/item relationship analysis and user/item classification). These concepts were then illustrated by a discussion of their practical applications in a variety of domains. Finally, we considered a number of different techniques used in evaluating the quality of recommender systems.

However, systems and techniques need to evolve over time, with the aim of improving performance, speed and proximity to the expectations or requirements of users. Several challenges remain to be met, for example:

– The improvement of collaborative filtering techniques, using more data sources (metadata or tagging data[1], demographic information, temporal data, etc.) or combining techniques that have yet to be used together.

– The volume of available data is constantly increasing and recommender systems encounter performance issues. They need to provide high-quality recommendations in record time in spite of this increase in data volume.

– Multi-criteria recommendation approaches (mentioned briefly in this book) are undergoing significant developments. The exploitation of multi-criteria scores, which contain contextual information, would be useful in improving recommendation quality.

– Contextual approaches (also mentioned briefly in this book) aim to take account of an individual's emotional context: for example, a person in love will find a romantic film more relevant than someone in a different emotional situation.

– Recommender systems use user data (profiles, etc.) to generate personalized recommendations. These systems attempt to collect as much data as possible. This may have a negative effect on user privacy (the system knows too much). Systems, therefore, need to make selective and reasonable use of user data and to guarantee a certain level of data security (non-disclosure, etc.).

In conclusion, recommender systems still need to respond to a number of different challenges. Developed in the context of a variety of research areas, they take a variety of forms and transcend specific disciplines. This field of research needs to remain as wide as possible in order to identify the most appropriate techniques and approaches for each specific application.

---

1 A tag is a keyword assigned to information (such as an image, an article or a video clip) describing a characteristic of the object, and makes it easier to group information containing the same keywords. Tags are selected arbitrarily and rarely form part of predefined sets of keywords.

Bibliography

[ABE 09] ABEL M.-H., LEBLANC A., "Knowledge sharing via the E-MEM0RAe2.0 platform", *6th International Conference on Intellectual Capital, Knowledge Management & Organisational Learning,* Montreal, Canada, pp. 10-19, October 2009.

[ADE 14] ADENIYI D., WAI Z., YONGQUAN Y., "Automated web usage data mining and recommendation system using k-nearest neighbor (KNN) classification method", *Applied Computing and Informatics,* 2014.

[ADO 05] ADOMAVICIUS G., TUZHILIN A., "Toward the next generation of recommender systems: a survey of the state-of-the-art and possible extensions", *IEEE Transactions on Knowledge and Data Engineering,* vol. 17, no. 6, pp. 734-749, 2005.

[ADO 08] ADOMAVICIUS G., TUZHILIN A., "Context-aware recommender systems", *Proceedings of the 2008 ACM Conference on Recommender Systems (RecSys '08),* New York, NY, ACM, pp. 335-336, 2008.

[AGR 93] AGRAWAL R., IMIELIŃSKI T., SWAMI A., "Mining association rules between sets of items in large databases", *ACM SIGMOD Record,* vol. 22, no. 2, pp. 207-216, June 1993.

[AMA 15] AMAZON, www.amazon.com, 2015.

[AND 08] ANDERSEN R., BORGS C., CHAYES J., *et al.,* "Trust-based recommendation systems: an axiomatic approach", *Proceedings of the 17th International Conference on World Wide Web (WWW '08),* New York, NY, ACM, pp. 199-208, 2008.

[ASS 14] ASSI R.A., ZARAKET F.A., MASRI W., "UCov: a user-defined coverage criterion for test case intent verification", *CoRR,* vol. abs/1407.3091, 2014.

[BAE 99] BAEZA-YATES R.A., RIBEIRO-NETO B., *Modern Information Retrieval,* Addison-Wesley Longman, Boston, MA, 1999.

[BAE 04] BAEZA-YATES R.A., HURTADO C.A., MENDOZA M., "Query recommendation using query logs in search engines", in LINDNER W., MESITI M., TÜRKER C., *et al.* (eds), *EDBT Workshops*, vol. 3268 of Lecture Notes in Computer Science, Springer, 2004-12-13, pp. 588-596, 2004.

[BAE 05] BAEZA-YATES R.A., HURTADO C.A., MENDOZA M., *et al.*, "Modeling user search behavior", *LA-WEB'05: Proceedings of the Third Latin American Web Congress*, Washington, DC, IEEE Computer Society, p. 242, 2005.

[BAK 05] BAKER K., Singular Value Decomposition Tutorial, 2005.

[BAL 97] BALABANOVIC M., SHOHAM Y., "Fab: content-based, collaborative recommendation", *Communications of the ACM*, vol. 40, no. 3, pp. 66-72, 1997.

[BAT 13] BATTY M., "Big data, smart cities and city planning", *Dialogues in Human Geography*, vol. 3, no. 3, pp. 274-279, 2013.

[BAV 10] BAVI V., BEIRNE T., BONE N., *et al.*, "Comparison of document similarity metrics", Computer Science Department, Western Washington University, Information Retrieval, Winter 2010, 2010.

[BEL 05] BELLATRECHE L., GIACOMETTI A., MARCEL P., *et al.*, "A personalization framework for OLAP queries", *ACM International Workshop on Datawarehousing and OLAP (DOLAP)*, pp. 9-18, 2005.

[BEN 07] BENNETT J., LANNING S., "The Netflix Prize", *Proceedings of the KDD Cup Workshop 2007*, New York, ACM, pp. 3-6, August 2007.

[BHA 91] BHATIA S.K., DEOGUN J.S., RAGHAVAN V.V., "User profiles for information retrieval", in RAS Z.W., ZEMANKOVA M. (eds), *ISMIS*, vol. 542 of Lecture Notes in Computer Science, Springer, pp. 102-111, 1991.

[BIL 98] BILLSUS D., PAZZANI M.J., "Learning collaborative information filters", *ICML'98: Proceedings of the Fifteenth International Conference on Machine Learning*, San Francisco, CA, Morgan Kaufmann, pp. 46-54, 1998.

[BIL 00] BILLSUS D., PAZZANI M.J., "User modeling for adaptive news access", *User Modeling and User-Adapted Interaction*, vol. 10, no. 2-3, pp. 147-180, 2000.

[BOH 07] BOHE S., RUMPLER B., "Modèle évolutif d'un profil utilisateur Application à la Recherche d'Information dans une bibliothèque numèrique de thèses", *CORIA*, pp. 197-209, March 2007.

[BRE 98] BREESE J.S., HECKERMAN D., KADIE C., "Empirical analysis of predictive algorithms for collaborative filtering", *Proceedings of the Fourteenth Conference on Uncertainty in Artificial Intelligence (UAI'98)*, San Francisco, CA, Morgan Kaufmann, pp. 43-52, 1998.

[BRU 11] BRULEY M., "Propos sur les SI Décisionnels", available at: http://www.expertbi.net/images/Docs/propos_sur_les_si_decisionnels.pdf, 2011.

[BUR 97] BURKE R.D., HAMMOND K.J., YOUNG B.C., "The FindMe approach to assisted browsing", *IEEE Expert*, vol. 12, pp. 32-40, 1997.

[BUR 00] BURKE R., "Knowledge-based recommender systems", in KENT A. (ed.), *Encyclopedia of Library and Information Science*, vol. 69, pp. 181-201, CRC Press, 2000.

[BUR 02] BURKE R., "Hybrid recommender systems: survey and experiments", *User Modeling and User-Adapted Interaction*, vol. 12, no. 4, pp. 331-370, November 2002.

[CAR 08] CARIOU V., CUBILLÉ J., DERQUENNE C., *et al.*, "Built-in indicators to discover interesting drill paths in a cube", *DaWaK*, pp. 33-44, 2008.

[CHA 09] CHATZOPOULOU G., EIRINAKI M., POLYZOTIS N., "Query recommendations for interactive database exploration", *SSDBM*, vol. 4, pp. 3-18, 2009.

[CHE 06] CHEN L., PU P., "Evaluating critiquing-based recommender agents", *Proceedings of the 21st National Conference on AAAI*, AAAI Press, pp. 157-162, 2006.

[CHU 93] CHUANG R.E., SHER D., "Chi^2 test for feature detection", *Pattern Recognition*, vol. 26, no 11, pp. 1671-1681, 1993.

[COV 06] COVER T., HART P., "Nearest neighbor pattern classification", *IEEE Transactions on Information Theory*, vol. 13, no. 1, pp. 21-27, September 2006.

[CRI 00] CRISTIANINI N., SHAWE-TAYLOR J., *An Introduction to Support Vector Machines and Other Kernel-based Learning Methods*, Cambridge University Press, New York, NY, 2000.

[DAO 08] DAOUD M., TAMINE L., BOUGHANEM M., *et al.*, "Construction des profils utilisateurs à base d'une ontologie pour une recherche d'information personnalisée", *Conférence francophone en Recherche d'information et Applications (CORIA)*, University of Rennes 1, pp. 225-240, March 2008.

[DEC 92] DECOURCY R., "Les systèmes d'information en réadaptation", *Réseau international CIDIH et facteurs environnementaux*, Québec, vols. 1-2, no. 5, pp. 7-10, 1992.

[DEE 90] DEERWESTER S., DUMAIS S.T., FURNAS G.W., *et al.*, "Indexing by latent semantic analysis", *Journal of the American Society for Information Science*, vol. 41, no. 6, pp. 391-407, 1990.

[DIC 45] DICE L.R., "Measures of the amount of ecologic association between species", *Ecology*, vol. 26, no. 3, pp. 297-302, July 1945.

[DJO 08] DJOUAD T., "Analyser l'activité d'apprentissage collaboratif: Une approche par transformations spécialisées de traces d'interactions", *Secondes Rencontres Jeunes Chercheurs en EIAH*, pp. 93-98, April 2008.

[EST 96] ESTER M., KRIEGEL P.H., SANDER J., *et al.*, "A density-based algorithm for discovering clusters in large spatial databases with noise", *Proceedings of the Second International Conference on ACM SIGKDD*, AAAI Press, pp. 226-231, 1996.

[FAC 15] FACEBOOK, https://www.facebook.com, 2015.

[FEL 08] FELFERNIG A., BURKE R., "Constraint-based recommender systems: technologies and research issues", *Proceedings of the 10th International Conference on Electronic Commerce (ICEC)*, New York, NY, ACM, pp. 3:1-3:10, 2008.

[FEL 07] FELFERNIG A., ISAK K., SZABO K., *et al.*, "The VITA financial services sales support environment", *Proceedings of the 19th National Conference on Innovative Applications of Artificial Intelligence*, AAAI Press, pp. 1692-1699, 2007.

[FER 13] FERRAGU E., *Modélisation des systèmes d'information décisionnels: techniques de modélisation conceptuelle et relationnelle des entrepôts de données*, Vuibert, 2013.

[FOD 02] FODOR I., A survey of dimension reduction techniques, Internal report, 2002.

[FOR 15] FORBES.COM, http://www.forbes.com, 2015.

[FRE 07] FREY B.J., DUECK D., "Clustering by passing messages between data points", *Science*, vol. 315, pp. 972-976, 2007.

[FRI 97] FRIEDMAN N., GEIGER D., GOLDSZMIDT M., "Bayesian network classifiers", *Machine Learning*, vol. 29, no. 2-3, pp. 131-163, November 1997.

[FU 02] FU Y., SHIH M.-Y., "A framework for personal web usage mining", *International Conference on Internet Computing*, pp. 595-600, 2002.

[GIA 09] GIACOMETTI A., MARCEL P., NEGRE E., "Recommending multidimensional queries", *DaWaK*, pp. 453-466, 2009.

[GIA 11] GIACOMETTI A., MARCEL P., NEGRE E., *et al.*, "Query recommendations for OLAP discovery-driven analysis", *IJDWM*, vol. 7, no. 2, pp. 1-25, 2011.

[GOL 65] GOLUB G., KAHAN W., "Calculating the singular values and pseudo-inverse of a matrix", *Journal of the Society for Industrial and Applied Mathematics Series B Numerical Analysis*, vol. 2, no. 2, pp. 205-224, 1965.

[GOL 70] GOLUB G.H., REINSCH C., "Singular value decomposition and least squares solutions", *Numerische Mathematik*, vol. 14, no. 5, pp. 403-420, April 1970.

[GOL 08] GOLBECK J., *Computing with Social Trust*, 1st edition, Springer, 2008.

[GOL 11] GOLFARELLI M., RIZZI S., BIONDI P., "myOLAP: an approach to express and evaluate OLAP preferences", *IEEE Transactions on Knowledge and Data Engineering*, vol. 23, no. 7, pp. 1050-1064, 2011.

[GUÉ 06] GUÉRIF S., Réduction de dimension en Apprentissage Numérique Non Supervisé, PhD thesis, University of Paris 13, 2006.

[GUT 00] GUTTA S., KURAPATI K., LEE K.P., *et al.*, "TV content recommender system", *Proceedings of the 17th National Conference on Artificial Intelligence and 12th Conference on Innovative Applications of Artificial Intelligence*, AAAI Press/MIT Press, pp. 1121-1122, 2000.

[HAR 79] HARTIGAN J.A., WONG M.A., "A k-means clustering algorithm", *JSTOR: Applied Statistics*, vol. 28, no. 1, pp. 100-108, 1979.

[HER 04] HERLOCKER J.L., KONSTAN J.A., TERVEEN L.G., *et al.*, "Evaluating collaborative filtering recommender systems", *ACM Transactions on Information Systems*, vol. 22, no. 1, pp. 5-53, January 2004.

[HER 08] HERNÁNDEZ F., GAUDIOSO E., "Evaluation of recommender systems: a new approach", *Expert Systems with Applications*, vol. 35, no. 3, pp. 790-804, October 2008.

[HIL 95] HILL W., STEAD L., ROSENSTEIN M., *et al.*, "Recommending and evaluating choices in a virtual community of use", *CHI'95: Proceedings of the SIGCHI Conference on Human Factors in Computing Systems*, New York, NY, ACM Press/Addison-Wesley, pp. 194-201, 1995.

[HUA 08] HUANG A., "Similarity measures for text document clustering", in HOLLAND J., NICHOLAS A., BRIGNOLI D. (eds), *New Zealand Computer Science Research Student Conference*, pp. 49-56, April 2008.

[HUA 04] HUANG Z., ZENG D., CHEN H., "A link analysis approach to recommendation under sparse data", *AMCIS, Association for Information Systems*, p. 239, 2004.

[INM 94] INMON W.H., HACKATHORN R.D., *Using the Data Warehouse*, Wiley-QED, Somerset, NJ, 1994.

[ISA 08] ISAKSSON A., WALLMAN M., GORANSSON H., *et al.*, "Cross-validation and bootstrapping are unreliable in small sample classification", *Pattern Recognition Letters*, vol. 29, no. 14, pp. 1960-1965, October 2008.

[JAI 88] JAIN A.K., DUBES R.C., *Algorithms for Clustering Data*, Prentice-Hall, Upper Saddle River, NJ, 1988.

[JAN 10] JANNACH D., ZANKER M., FELFERNIG A., *et al.*, *Recommender Systems: An Introduction*, 1st edition, Cambridge University Press, New York, NY, 2010.

[JÄR 02] JÄRVELIN K., KEKÄLÄINEN J., "Cumulated gain-based evaluation of IR techniques", *ACM Transactions on Information Systems*, vol. 20, no. 4, pp. 422-446, October 2002.

[JER 09] JERBI H., RAVAT F., TESTE O., *et al.*, "Preference-based recommendations for OLAP analysis", *DaWaK,* pp. 467-478, 2009.

[KAZ 06] KAZIENKO P., KOLODZIEJSKI P., "Personalized integration of recommendation methods for e-commerce", *IJCSA*, vol. 3, no. 3, pp. 12-26, 2006.

[KEN 71] KENT A., *Information Analysis and Retrieval*, John Wiley and Sons, 1971.

[KHO 09] KHOUSSAINOVA N., BALAZINSKA M., GATTERBAUER W., *et al.*, "A case for a collaborative query management system", *CIDR: Proceedings of the 4th Biennial Conference on Innovative Data Systems Research*, Asilomar, CA, 2009.

[KIM 02] KIMBALL R., ROSS M., *The Data Warehouse Toolkit: The Complete Guide to Dimensional Modeling*, 2nd edition, John Wiley and Sons, New York, NY, 2002.

[KOR 09] KOREN Y., The BellKor Solution to the Netflix Grand Prize, available at: www.netflix.com/assets/GrandPrize2009_BPC_BellKor.pdf, 2009.

[KOU 04] KOUTRIKA G., IOANNIDIS Y., "Personalization of queries in database systems", *Proceedings of the 20th International Conference on Data Engineering (ICDE)*, Washington, DC, IEEE Computer Society, pp. 597-609, 2004.

[LAH 03] LAHLOU A., URIEN P., "SIM-filter: user profile based smart information filtering and personalization in smartcard", *The 15th Conference on Advanced Information Systems Engineering (CAiSE)*, Austria, 16-20 June, 2003.

[LAK 11] LAKIOTAKI K., MATSATSINIS N., TSOUKIÀS A., "Multicriteria user modeling in recommender systems", *Intelligent Systems*, IEEE, vol. 26, no. 2, pp. 64-76, March 2011.

[LAS 15] LAST.FM, http://www.last.fm, 2015.

[LI 13] LI Q., Modeling and exploitation of the traces of interactions in the collaborative working environment, Thesis, University of Technology of Compiègne, July 2013.

[LIN 02] LIN W., ALVAREZ S.A., RUIZ C., "Efficient adaptive-support association rule mining for recommender systems", *Data Mining and Knowledge Discovery*, vol. 6, no. 1, pp. 83-105, January 2002.

[LIN 03] LINDEN G., SMITH B., YORK J., "Amazon.com recommendations: item-to-item collaborative filtering", *Internet Computing,* IEEE, vol. 7, no. 1, pp. 76-80, January 2003.

[LIN 98] LING C., LING C.X., LI C., "Data mining for direct marketing: problems and solutions", *Proceedings of the Fourth International Conference on Knowledge Discovery and Data Mining (KDD)*, AAAI Press, pp. 73-79, 1998.

[LIN 15] LINKEDIN, https://www.linkedin.com, 2015.

[LYM 03] LYMAN P., VARIAN H.R., CHARLES P., *et al.*, "How much information?", available at: http://www2.sims.berkeley.edu/research/projects/how-much-info-2003, 2003.

[MAN 94] MANNILA H., TOIVONEN H., VERKAMO I., *Efficient Algorithms for Discovering Association Rules*, AAAI Press, 1994.

[MAN 08] MANNING C.D., RAGHAVAN P., SCHÜTZE H., *Introduction to Information Retrieval*, Cambridge University Press, New York, NY, 2008.

[MAR 11] MARCEL P., NEGRE E., "A survey of query recommendation techniques for datawarehouse exploration", *EDA*, 2011.

[MCL 11] MCLUHAN M., GORDON W., *Counterblast 1954*, Gingko Press, 2011.

[MCS 04] MCSHERRY D., "Maximally successful relaxations of unsuccessful queries", *15th Conference on Artificial Intelligence and Cognitive Science*, Galway, Ireland, pp. 127-136, 2004.

[MIR 05] MIRZADEH N., RICCI F., BANSAL M., "Feature selection methods for conversational recommender systems", *IEEE Computer Society*, pp. 772-777, 2005.

[NEG 09] NEGRE E., Collaborative exploration of data cubes, PhD thesis, University François-Rabelais, Tours, France, 2009.

[NEG 13] NEGRE E., "Towards a knowledge (experience)-based recommender system for crisis management", *Eighth International Conference on P2P, Parallel, Grid, Cloud and Internet Computing (3PGCIC)*, Compiegne, France, October 28-30, pp. 713-718, 2013.

[NEG 14] NEGRE E., ROSENTHAL-SABROUX C., "Recommendations to improve the smartness of a city", in DAMERI R.P., ROSENTHAL-SABROUX C. (eds), *Smart City, Progress in IS*, Springer, 2014.

[NET 15] NETFLIX, https://www.netflix.com, 2015.

[OLS 95] OLSON C.F., "Parallel algorithms for hierarchical clustering", *Parallel Computing*, vol. 21, pp. 1313-1325, 1995.

[PAZ 07] PAZZANI M.J., BILLSUS D., "The adaptive Web", *Chapter Content-based Recommendation Systems*, pp. 325-341, Springer-Verlag, Berlin, 2007.

[PEA 01] PEARSON K., "On lines and planes of closest fit to systems of points in space", *Philosophical Magazine*, vol. 2, no. 6, pp. 559-572, 1901.

[PIE 03] PIERRAKOS D., PALIOURAS G., PAPATHEODOROU C., *et al.*, "Web usage mining as a tool for personalization: a survey", *User Modeling and User-Adapted Interaction*, vol. 13, no. 4, pp. 311-372, November 2003.

[PYL 99] PYLE D., *Data Preparation for Data Mining*, Morgan Kaufmann, San Francisco, CA, 1999.

[QAM 10] QAMAR A.M., Generalized cosine and similarity metrics: a supervised learning approach based on nearest neighbors, Thesis, University of Grenoble, November 2010.

[QUI 86] QUINLAN J.R., "Induction of decision trees", *Machine Learning*, vol. 1, no. 1, pp. 81-106, March 1986.

[QUI 93] QUINLAN J.R., *C4.5: Programs for Machine Learning*, Morgan Kaufmann, San Francisco, CA, 1993.

[RIC 07] RICCI F., NGUYEN Q.N., "Acquiring and revising preferences in a critique-based mobile recommender system", *IEEE Intelligent Systems*, vol. 22, no. 3, pp. 22-29, 2007.

[RIC 11] RICCI F., ROKACH L., SHAPIRA B., *et al.* (eds), *Recommender Systems Handbook*, Springer, 2011.

[ROC 71] ROCCHIO J.J., "Relevance feedback in information retrieval", in SALTON G. (ed.), *The Smart Retrieval System – Experiments in Automatic Document Processing*, pp. 313-323, Prentice-Hall, Englewood Cliffs, NJ, 1971.

[ROD 88] RODGERS J.L., NICEWANDER A.W., "Thirteen ways to look at the correlation coefficient", *The American Statistician*, vol. 42, no. 1, pp. 59-66, 1988.

[ROK 08] ROKACH L., MAIMON O., *Data Mining with Decision Trees: Theory and Applications*, World Scientific Publishing, River Edge, NJ, 2008.

[ROS 09] ROSENTHAL-SABROUX C., CARVALHO A., *Management et gouvernance des SI*, Hermès-Lavoisier, Paris, 2009.

[ROY 96] ROY B., *Multicriteria Methodology for Decision Aiding*, Kluwer Academic, Dordrecht, 1996.

[SAL 75] SALTON G., WONG A., YANG C.S., "A vector space model for automatic indexing", *Communications of the ACM*, vol. 18, no. 11, pp. 613-620, November 1975.

[SAL 83] SALTON G., *Introduction to Modern Information Retrieval*, McGraw-Hill, September 1983.

[SAP 99] SAPIA C., "On modeling and predicting query behavior in OLAP systems", *DMDW*, p. 2, 1999.

[SAR 00] SARAWAGI S., "User-adaptive exploration of multidimensional data", *VLDB*, pp. 307-316, 2000.

[SCH 90] SCHRAGE M., *Shared Minds: The New Technologies of Collaboration*, Random House, New York, NY, 1990.

[SCH 01] SCHAFER J.B., KONSTAN J.A., RIEDL J., "E-commerce recommendation applications", *Data Mining and Knowledge Discovery*, vol. 5, no. 1/2, pp. 115-153, 2001.

[SCH 07] SCHAFER J.B., FRANKOWSKI D., HERLOCKER J., *et al.*, "The adaptive Web", *Chapter Collaborative Filtering Recommender Systems*, pp. 291-324, Springer-Verlag, Berlin, 2007.

[SMY 04] SMYTH B., MCGINTY L., REILLY J., *et al.*, "Compound critiques for conversational recommender systems", *WI'04: Proceedings of the 2004 IEEE/WIC/ACM International Conference on Web Intelligence*, Washington, DC, IEEE Computer Society, pp. 145-151, 2004.

[SRI 00] SRIVASTAVA J., COOLEY R., DESHPANDE M., *et al.*, "Web usage mining: discovery and applications of usage patterns from Web data", *SIGKDD Explorations*, vol. 1, no. 2, pp. 12-23, 2000.

[STA 92] STAIR R.M., *Principles of Information Systems: A Managerial Approach*, Course Technology Press, Boston, MA, 1992.

[STE 09] STEFANIDIS K., DROSOU M., PITOURA E., "You may also like results in relational databases", *Proceedings of PersDB 2009, in Conjunction with the VLDB 2009 Conference*, Lyon, France, 2009.

[STR 00] STREHL A., GHOSH J., MOONEY R., "Impact of similarity measures on Web-page clustering", *Proceedings of the 17th National Conference on Artificial Intelligence: Workshop of Artificial Intelligence for Web Search (AAAI)*, July 30-31, Austin, TX, pp. 58-64, 2000.

[TCH 12] TCHUENTE D., PÉNINOU A., JESSEL N., *et al.*, "Modélisation générique du processus de développement des profils utilisateurs dans les systèmes d'information (regular paper)", *Colloque Veille Stratégique Scientifique et Technologique (VSST)*, Université Paul Sabatier, Toulouse, May 2012.

[THO 04] THOMPSON C.A., GÖKER M., LANGLEY P., "A personalized system for conversational recommendations", *Journal of Artificial Intelligence Research*, vol. 21, pp. 393-428, 2004.

[UNG 98] UNGAR L., FOSTER D., ANDRE E., *et al.*, *Clustering Methods for Collaborative Filtering*, AAAI Press, 1998.

[VII 14] VIITANEN J., KINGSTON R., "Smart cities and green growth: outsourcing democratic and environmental resilience to the global technology sector", *Environment and Planning A*, vol. 46, no. 4, pp. 803-819, April 2014.

[WAI 10] WAIDYANATHA N., "Towards a typology of integrated functional early warning systems", *International Journal of Critical Infrastructures*, vol. 6, no. 1, pp. 31-51, 2010.

[WAN 14] WANG N., ABEL M.-H., BARTHES J.-P., *et al.*, "Towards a recommender system from semantic traces for decision aid", *International Conference on Knowledge Management and Information Sharing (KMIS)*, Rome, Italy, pp. 274-280, 2014.

[WAN 15] WANG N., ABEL M.-H., BARTHES J.-P., *et al.*, "Mining user competency from semantic trace", *ACM Conference on Computer-Supported Cooperative Work and Social Computing (CCSCW)*, Italy, 2015.

[WHI 07] WHITE R.W., BILENKO M., CUCERZAN S., "Studying the use of popular destinations to enhance web search interaction", *SIGIR*, pp. 159-166, 2007.

[WIK 15a] WIKIPEDIA, "Information and communications technology", en.wikipedia.org/wiki/Information_and_communications_technology, 2015.

[WIK 15b] WIKISTAT.FR, "Introduction à l'analyse en composantes principales (ACP)", http://wikistat.fr/pdf/st-l-descript-estim-intro.pdf, March 2015.

[YAN 09] YANG X., PROCOPIUC C.M., SRIVASTAVA D., "Recommending join queries via query log analysis", *ICDE*, pp. 964-975, 2009.

[ZAR 11] ZARKA R., CORDIER A., EGYED-ZSIGMOND E., *et al.*, "Trace replay with change propagation impact in client/server applications", in MILLE A. (ed.), *Ingénierie des connaissances (IC)*, Publibook, May 2011.

[ZIE 05] ZIEGLER C.-N., MCNEE S.M., KONSTAN J.A., *et al.*, "Improving recommendation lists through topic diversification", *Proceedings of the 14th International Conference on World Wide Web (WWW)*, New York, NY, ACM, pp. 22-32, 2005.

[ZUR 92] ZURADA J. M., *Introduction to Artificial Neural Systems*, West Publishing, 1992.

Index

Other titles from

in

Information Systems, Web and Pervasive Computing

2015

ARDUIN Pierre-Emmanuel, GRUNDSTEIN Michel,
ROSENTHAL-SABROUX Camille
Information and Knowledge System

BÉRANGER Jérôme
Medical Information Systems Ethics

IAFRATE Fernando
From Big Data to Smart Data

POMEROL Jean-Charles, EPELBOIN Yves, THOURY Claire
MOOCs

SALLES Maryse
Decision-Making and the Information System

2014

DINET Jérôme
Information Retrieval in Digital Environments

HÉNO Raphaële, CHANDELIER Laure
3D Modeling of Buildings: Outstanding Sites

Thériault Marius, des Rosiers François
Modeling Urban Dynamics

2009

Bonnet Pierre, Detavernier Jean-Michel, Vauquier Dominique
Sustainable IT Architecture: the Progressive Way of Overhauling Information Systems with SOA

Papy Fabrice
Information Science

Rivard François, Abou Harb Georges, Meret Philippe
The Transverse Information System

Roche Stéphane, Caron Claude
Organizational Facets of GIS

Ventre Daniel
Information Warfare

2008

Brugnot Gérard
Spatial Management of Risks

Finke Gerd
Operations Research and Networks

Guermond Yves
Modeling Process in Geography

Kanevski Michael
Advanced Mapping of Environmental Data

Manouvrier Bernard, Laurent Ménard
Application Integration: EAI, B2B, BPM and SOA

Papy Fabrice
Digital Libraries

2007

DOBESCH Hartwig, DUMOLARD Pierre, DYRAS Izabela
Spatial Interpolation for Climate Data

SANDERS Lena
Models in Spatial Analysis

2006

CLIQUET Gérard
Geomarketing

CORNIOU Jean-Pierre
Looking Back and Going Forward in IT

DEVILLERS Rodolphe, JEANSOULIN Robert
Fundamentals of Spatial Data Quality

CPSIA information can be obtained at www.ICGtesting.com
Printed in the USA
BVOW06s1024240915

419426BV00011B/33/P